KENNEDY'S

POCKET GUIDE

TO WORKING

WITH

EXECUTIVE

RECRUITERS

KENNEDY INFORMATION

Compiled and published by Kennedy Information, Inc.
A subsidiary of The Bureau of National Affairs, Inc.

Publishers of **Executive Recruiter News, Recruiting Trends,
The Directory of Executive Recruiters, The International Directory of
Executive Recruiters, The Directory of Outplacement and Career
Management Firms** and **Recruiting Solutions Conference and Expo**
One Phoenix Mill Lane, 5th Fl., Peterborough, NH 03458
603-924-1006, FAX 603-924-4460
E-mail: bookstore@kennedyinfo.com, www.KennedyInfo.com
ISBN 1-885922-38-8, Price: $17.95

ABOUT THIS GUIDE . . .

When our first *Directory of Executive Recruiters* was published in 1971, it was a rather thin 52-page booklet plainly listing some 450 firms.

By the second edition, however, we were beginning to recognize the need to provide some guidance on how to use the list and how to work with the recruiters. Our response was a single page of text outlining a few cautions!

Over the years we have continuously expanded and refined this text portion: it grew to over 100 pages of helpful information from a wide variety of sources.

But with the entire directory at over 1,000 pages and more than two inches thick, we were approaching the physical limits of binding in paperback form.

Besides, we found that many directory purchasers skipped directly to the listings and missed all the up-front text! And purchasers of the listings in our disk format wouldn't be getting the text at all. So we decided to separate the how-to-use information from the search firm listings and their extensive cross-indexes. Thus was born this companion to *The Directory of Executive Recruiters*, useful for anyone serious about his or her career.

This new edition of the "pocket" guide has added considerably to the expertise of the first. There are over 170 pages covering, we hope, the gamut of information and guidance needed to have successful relationships with executive recruiters. We are especially appreciative of the cooperation of our contributors, who have made this unique publication possible, and we welcome comments and suggestions from job-changers to help us make the next edition even better.

TABLE OF CONTENTS

Other Resources from Kennedy Information

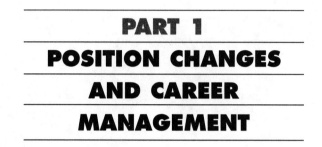

PART 1
POSITION CHANGES
AND CAREER
MANAGEMENT

CHAPTER 1
SEARCHING FOR A NEW POSITION

The unexamined life is not worth living.
– Socrates (c 470-399 b.c.)

Y ou are reading this book because either you've decided to change jobs or you think you might need to or want to change jobs. This book is designed to help you make the decisions necessary to initiate a position change and then to work successfully with executive recruiters to help make it happen. This chapter and the next prepare you to make key decisions and to start the job-search campaign.

CHANGING JOBS

Changing jobs is never easy, even when the change is welcome. The perfect dream job will still bring with it headaches and growing pains like paperwork, possible relocation, financial changes, as well as the pressure of learning the ins and outs of a new position. Meanwhile, there are the deeper uncertainties of your family's security, your ability to perform at the new job, and wondering if your career (and even your life) is meaningful. When the change comes from a layoff or other unexpected job loss, these concerns are only intensified.

Since the job-changing process is difficult enough itself, you want to make it as worthwhile as possible and be sure that you have all the bases covered. It's a miserable experience to make a major life decision too quickly, only to discover too late it was the wrong one. The grass always seems to be greener on the other side of the fence, but sometimes it really isn't. The best way to give yourself an advantage in a job change is to be as informed as you can about the market, what you have to offer it, and most importantly, what it can offer you. Yes, times are harder than they were during the Internet boom, but good candidates still have many choices of career paths. Even if you are pressed for time or money because of a layoff, you still need to be as thorough as possible while considering your options. This means evaluating your current situation, what you want from your future job, and then taking steps to getting it.

Changing Jobs vs. Changing Careers

Before going forward, it's important to distinguish between changing a job, or position, and changing a career. The differences are not entirely black and white, but for the most part, changing a job means moving to a different position within your current field or finding a type of job that you may never have held before, but that still requires the basic background and skill set you possess. An example would be changing from selling pharmaceuticals to selling insurance. Yes, pharmaceuticals and insurance are two different fields, but selling either still involves customer prospecting, customer service, account management, travel, and the like.

Changing a career, on the other hand, implies that you are completely changing your entire work field: for example, leaving the marketing world to become a teacher, or quitting a sales job to start a nonprofit. Changing a career demands deep soul-searching and can be extremely labor- and time-intensive, sometimes requiring several years to learn a new set of skills, go back to school, or even taking a pay cut to start all over again and begin a field at entry-level. The trade-off, however, is that ideally you are changing careers to do something you love, and this makes up for the steps back you may have to take.

For the purpose of this book, we will focus mainly on changing jobs, assuming that you already have an idea of, and the requisite experience for, the position you are seeking. While the advice we give can certainly be applied to a career change as well, the executive recruiting process can be best utilized for making a job or position change into another company. Executive recruiters will be interested in you only if your skills and experience match the jobs you want. If you desire a complete career change, it might be better first to do your soul-searching and decide what you want that new career to be. Then, if you have the right skills, or can learn them through schooling or working in the field even "pro bono" (for free) to gain experience, you can consider a recruiter.

Do You Really Need to Change Jobs?

You may have days when you want nothing more than to slam shut your laptop and stride out the door for good. Or, like Ed, you generally like your job, but you have a sense of malaise that you just can't shake and you don't know why. There are times when we all feel that another job–any job–would be better than what we've got. But if you look again, you may find that the reason you are down about your job is not the work itself, but surrounding circumstances.

So before you take your job and shove it, ask yourself why you want to change in the first place. It might be a common and correctable situation. Following are some common and often remedied situations, usually worth an attempt to fix before jumping ship. If the corrections prove elusive, however, a job search may be in order.

I liked being a Web development manager, and my salary was good enough, but the overall job was just so dull. It was quiet, and everyone was very structured and serious. Then we landed a big client, and the marketing team needed someone to manage that account. I volunteered. Basically, I had the same job, just moved to a different cubicle, with more relaxed people. Suddenly I really enjoyed coming into work every day."

– Ed, 32, Annapolis, Maryland

You Want a Higher Salary

We all like to say that it's not about the money but that the work is meaningful. And for many that is true. But the truth is, in the real world, if the money isn't what it should be, we aren't going to be happy. That's not to say every job has to have a high salary, but it does need to be in accordance with the job description and your experience. Obviously, if you are still new to a field or a company, you can't expect to be top guy or gal on the totem pole just yet. But if you believe that you deserve more, don't change jobs to get it without asking for more at your current job first.

It's fairly simple to determine the worth of your position. There are many salary calculators on the Web that give you salaries appropriate for your field, level and region. You can also get feedback from professional organizations for your field. Then determine your worth by adding up the basic salary as well as your own personal accomplishments and experience. Document these numbers along with your accomplishments. Speak in bottom-line terms: "I did X, and therefore brought Y amount of revenue to the company." Also have copies of your reviews handy and any other praise you have received.

After doing your homework, set a time with your manager, present why you deserve more pay, and ask for it. Be sure to have a strong case, for a weak one can be an embarrassment and can make your relationship with your superiors more difficult. If the answer is no, try asking for a portion now and a portion later, or something equally valuable to you, like tuition assistance or extra vacation days. Good employees are very hard (and expensive) to replace, so don't be sheepish–but do be reasonable. And if you still aren't satisfied, now you already have a good figure in mind to ask for at your next job.

The Thrill Is Gone

Maybe, like Ed, you enjoy what you do, but not where you do it. Or maybe you like your company, but have outgrown your job and are bored. Perhaps your personality is just different from your co-workers; you are an outgoing people person, while they are more content to keep to themselves. The chemistry isn't there.

Can you fix this situation? You may try migrating within your organization. Analyze your transferable skills, such as managing people, project management, sales skills, and communication skills. This type of experience can be applied across various departments. Get involved in projects that are outside of your comfort zone; this will give you a chance to flex some different job muscles. You may do a complete internal transfer, or you may find yourself working in the same organizational unit but with different people. Also check internal job listings, and ask your human resources department about other openings; it's much easier for them to hire from within than to bring in an outsider. Ultimately you will either find a position in your current company that you enjoy more or, at the very least, gain experience to help you land another job outside the company. Either way is a growth experience. If such a crossover can't be achieved, it's probably time to move on.

Difficult Boss or Co-Workers

Even though we are adults, to answer the classic question, no, we can't all just get along. Every workplace will have its difficult personalities. Aside from the more serious issues of sexual harassment or workplace bullying/violence (which require investigation and assistance), there are ways to learn to deal with co-workers—or at least tolerate them. Bosses may be in the same category. If you love everything else about your job, then you would do well to try to solve the problem before just quitting. (Who knows what types of boss or co-workers you will encounter at your next job anyway?)

For some, being upfront is the best way to go about resolving conflict. Sometimes you can ease tension by sitting down with someone you dislike and having a heart-to-heart talk with them, either just the two of you or with another manager present. Or you could try the good Samaritan approach and take the person out to lunch to try to find other common ground besides work.

Also, consider this—difficult as it may be: could the problem be you? While you may not agree with the boss or co-worker you dislike, there may be a grain of truth in their problem with you. Have you had a history of conflict with co-workers in the past? Ask your close friends and family members for their honest opinion of how you relate to people. In the end, the best course of action may be just to get over it. Really. You can't change people, and you like your job. You'll have to decide if there's a reasonable opportunity to recover a productive relationship and if it's serious enough to escape if you can't.

Lack of Advancement

Perhaps you have been with your company for a long time, but you haven't moved up the way you would like. Maybe you feel there is nowhere to go. Ask yourself what you have done to make a promotion happen. Have you called attention to your successes? Have you asked to move up, or have you waited for other people to make the decision? Are your skills up to date?

Maybe it's just your division that has no upward mobility, but you could get higher on the ladder by switching departments. Or perhaps you could find an entirely different job within your division or company. Again, there are ways to completely redirect your path without leaving a company. Keep in mind as you consider a job search the job market is kinder to people with an upward trajectory. Executive recruiters are especially focused on these people. If your career ascendancy is slowing or non-existent, that may well signal a change.

Buying Time

If you're indecisive about whether to stay or go, there are other steps you can take to buy yourself some time and recharge your life both in and out of work. It's better to proceed with caution than just to quit without knowing at all what you want to do. And it is better to grow somehow than not to grow at all. The job market can be unforgiving toward people who give up.

Going back to school is one route many professionals take these days. It could be for an MBA or a degree related to your work directly. Or it could be in photography or writing—one of those creative, dream jobs you've always wanted. Can you get tuition assistance? Take online classes? In today's modern workplace it might be possible to scale back your hours each week or work from home one day of the week. Even though you are working, just being in your home environment a little more might make for more peace of mind.

Take a vacation, and use the time to refresh and consider your possibilities. You might even be able to arrange a sabbatical, a period of time off without pay. Work freelance or part-time, or volunteer in a field you might want to explore. It can recharge you, help you make contacts, and give you a chance to spread your wings without having to leave the nest. If you plan it right, have a good goal and achieve it, such career interludes can be very productive and lead to other good career events.

WHEN YOU KNOW IT'S TIME TO GO

Now that you've assessed your situation, you may realize that your job problems can't be easily fixed, or fixed without major investments or risks you're not willing to take. And sometimes it's just plain obvious–corrective actions are likely to be a waste of time. Your personal and career life is sinking together. It becomes emotional–and even physical. You can't sleep and feel like you've aged 10 years in the last two. The following are hard to fix, and if you fall into one of these next situations, it's definitely time to move on.

Burnout

You hate getting up to go to work. Sunday evenings you become depressed. You drowse through meetings, procrastinate over even the simplest of tasks. You come in late and sneak out early. Nothing about your job excites you anymore. Worst of all, your performance suffers and you just don't care anymore about performance or what people think of you. You are just plain burnt out. Job burnout is a common phenomenon, so you shouldn't feel guilty about it. You should, however, correct it quickly. You still owe your company (and more importantly yourself) a good performance for as long as you remain at that company. You don't want to engage in a job search–or work with recruiters–with too much excess negative baggage from your current situation.

You're on the Wrong Track

Before St. Louis Rams quarterback Kurt Warner became the 1999 Super Bowl MVP, he had been stocking shelves in an Iowa supermarket. It took great courage and hard work on his part to give football one more shot, but it paid off big-time.

Perhaps you took a job with your company just out of college and never had a chance to try other opportunities. Maybe you have had family commitments that haven't allowed you to explore your interests. Or you may actually have done very well in your field and been promoted so often that you never had a chance to stop and really look at what you are doing and whether it makes you happy or not. After all, you will spend some 80,000 hours of your life at work; you should do something that you enjoy. The sooner you change directions in your career track, the sooner you can pursue something that really matters to you.

Stress Is Taking Its Toll

Of course business travel is frustrating, and your boss may be a pain in the neck. But if these sorts of things are manifesting themselves as health problems for you, you must change something. No job is worth compromising your health, and you may also have a family to think of as well. Finding a better position can help you feel better physically, mentally and spiritually.

Can Golden Handcuffs Be Unlocked?

You may face the "golden handcuffs"–compensation, benefits and other economic factors compelling you to stay on, particularly near retirement. You may be frustrated knowing that you dislike your job and would like to leave, but you are only a few years from a clean break such as retirement. Only you can make that decision. Perhaps it is worth it now to slug out a few more years in order to retire better–nothing wrong with thinking long-term. You may also be bound by your family's needs–again this is your call. If financial concerns are the only problem, you might want to sit down with a financial planner and see what can be done. Do you have to stay in order to receive a pension, or can you take your money and roll it over to an IRA? Are you working a job you hate on the off chance that the company's stock options might hit it big someday? Are you fully vested? Now is the time to look at your portfolio–and that of your spouse as well–to see where you are. You might be surprised to find that you can change jobs with less risk than you thought.

Outside Signals

Whether you work at a start-up or a longtime, established company, at some point your company will face tough times. It could just be a down cycle, or it could be a signal that worse times are coming. Keep informed of your company's progress and financial status, as well as that of similar companies, and you will be in a better position to know how its ups and downs can affect your job. Even if you love what you do and where you are, if other companies in your sector are laying people off in droves, you want to be prepared now should your company go the same route. Or if your company is smaller and is struggling to get funding to launch its products or to establish a stable management team, you might also want to begin looking elsewhere. Always keep your resume and contacts updated and check periodically the job openings in your field. There's nothing wrong with facing the challenge of turning a company around, but you can't do it alone. Don't ever think layoffs can't happen to you.

Greenlighting.

When companies merge, this is the signal given to the manager to start looking because his or her counterpart in the other company will assume the role for the combined firm.

Recruiters advise not waiting until it's too late. They and their hiring client companies understand economic cycles and downturns. But having said that, unemployed people are often considered "damaged goods" by clients and recruiters alike and are eliminated from job searches. It is no doubt harder to go the recruiter route if you're unemployed, and, if you anticipate downsizing, it's best to head for the lifeboats–get started building recruiter relationships and starting your job search–before the ship goes down.

On the other hand, you and your company may be doing well, but you keep hearing about other great jobs. Recruiters are calling you, and that company that went public last year continues to perform well and produce products that interest you. This is another signal that you may want to move on. When the sun shines, make hay. It's risky, sure, but the greatest risk you can take in life is never taking one at all. You may get a better job and you may also build a lasting recruiter relationship that can pay dividends in future career moves.

EASING A CAREER TRANSITION

Now suppose you find another job you are interested in. Interviews are done and it appears you have the inside track for the job. Now is the best time to begin thinking about making the change.

A Team Effort

But before saying yes, do a serious evaluation of the job itself. Is it really worth the change you are about to make? Are you accepting it for the right reasons; in other words, are you letting a high salary cloud your judgment as to whether it really is a good position for you? Make a chart, write down the pros and cons, talk to people close to you. It's like buying a new car, only more so.

You also must sit down with your family before you make such a decision, especially if the job means a serious life change for them, like relocation. Is your spouse willing to leave his or her job to accompany you without resentment? Are your children established in school and community programs from which leaving could be detrimental? You may also have elderly relatives that need your care. You must take all of these things into consideration.

Time and Attitude

Maybe you have been laid off and you've taken an unfamiliar position out of necessity. Or perhaps you've purposely taken on a job change and found something better. Either way, time and attitude are the keys to easing a job or career transition.

The more time you can take between jobs the better. Time gives you a chance to breathe, to rest, to adjust, and to get your affairs in order. Perhaps you and your family can take a vacation. You want to be able to begin your new job refreshed. Try to arrange enough time off between jobs, and be firm about your start date.

Time is also something you must be willing to give to the new job. While job changing is much more common and accepted today than it was 10 years ago, job hopping every few months has never been in vogue. You need to be able to give at least a year to the new job; committing to that will not only help you perform better but will look better on your resume if you choose to leave down the road.

Keep a positive attitude. New jobs bring many humbling lessons that can be even worse if it is a job you aren't especially happy about. Don't expect to be ahead of the learning curve. You may be taking orders from younger people and having to learn some basic skills. Try to be thankful for the job and know that one day you will be at the level you need to be. Continue to keep your job options open, and stay in touch with your contacts. Having just come off of a job search, you know how difficult it can be to find leads and references if you have let relationships lapse. Don't make the same mistake again.

Housekeeping

As you leave your current position, be sure to stay on top of all your paperwork. Get it signed, sealed and delivered before you leave. If you put it off, you won't have time or energy to deal with it at your new job (which will also have paperwork of its own). Also, contact your legal counsel to review any agreements or contracts with which you are uncomfortable.

Follow through with exit interviews, and no matter what, do not bad-mouth your former boss, co-workers, or the company. It is never a good idea to burn bridges, especially in today's economy where companies that used to compete are now merging. You never know when you might wind up working with a former co-worker again. Other companies find out, and recruiters find out through the grapevine, and nobody wants to take a chance on a bad attitude.

Also, be willing to help train your replacement to ease the transitions. Your company may want to rehire you someday as a full-time worker or a contractor, so it only helps you to be as cooperative as possible.

Get your personal financial life in order. Talk to your financial planner to begin necessary rollovers. You don't want your money sitting idle during the changeover. Look into reinvesting it into your new company's pension plan or a retirement account of your own.

And be discreet. Don't linger in the coffee room discussing your departure or go on and on about your exciting new opportunity. Until the moment you walk out the door, continue to act and work as if you will be a longtime employee of your current company.

Finally, if you're working with an executive recruiter, it is to your advantage to maintain the relationship. Do what you can to keep in touch. No position is permanent (unless you're a Supreme Court Justice)–someday, sooner or later, you may want the recruiter's services once again. Keep the recruiter advised of your job transition and your career progress. It's always good to have someone outside your organization keep an interest in your career progress. But maybe this is getting ahead a little. The next few chapters will guide you through starting a job search–and the role executive recruiters can play in your quest for a new position.

CHAPTER 2
STARTING YOUR JOB SEARCH

A resume is like a snowflake: highly individualized and painfully short-lived . . . but best used in large quantities. The statistical chances of a few resumes producing results are so miniscule as to justify mass distribution to all likely targets in most cases.
– James H. Kennedy, founding editor of *Executive Recruiter News*

The "discovery" phase is over. You've analyzed your current career situation and have decided superficial fixes won't work; something more needs to be done. You're ready to change jobs. Congratulations! You probably feel excited, knowing that an important shift is about to take place in your life–and you should. As long as you develop an effective strategy ahead of time and use the wealth of assistance that is available to you, you may just find that the job-search process can be not only empowering, even oddly enjoyable, but can help you learn things about yourself that can be applied in areas of your life outside of work as well.

A PLAN OF ATTACK

Ideally, you have been monitoring your career all along, researching other fields and companies, keeping your resume updated, nurturing your contacts. If so, beginning a job search won't be difficult–your hardest work is already done. Recruiters may have contacted you already because you have been adept at maintaining your contacts.

Unfortunately, most of us are not that good about keeping up. We're so focused on our current position, even if we don't like it, that we fail to maintain the valuable research necessary to find our next "big thing." Or if we do like our current job, we become lax and comfortable, not expecting to leave–until we are laid off. The fact is, whether it is for your own job safety or to discover other fields in which you might be happier, it's always good to make the job search an ongoing process.

The good news is that you have a wealth of strategies and tools for a career search; however, so many options can be overwhelming. It's easy, especially if time and money are scarce, to panic and be led off your path to a dream position. Who has time for that? But you wouldn't go in to lead a meeting without an agenda or build a house without a blueprint, would you? If you have a plan of action, you'll be better able to conduct your search.

To get the most out of your job search, the next steps are to evaluate yourself and your job-search options. Then you build your search strategy and start executing that strategy. And because an executive recruiter can be a crucial part of that strategy, it's good to start understanding now how one can help you.

GETTING YOURSELF IN GEAR

After making the big decision, the next big step is to start preparing yourself for the search, to get yourself ready. If you're planning to sell a car, you want to get everything fixed and cleaned up before placing the ad, right? No last minute dashes to the auto detailer or repair shop. Murphy and his law will be laying in wait. Things will go wrong, money will be spent, buyer appointments will be missed, and you'll carry off the look of being disorganized and hiding bigger problems with last minute fixes. It's better–and it feels better–to prepare well in advance, even before making your first contact with a prospective employer or recruiter.

Attitude Check

Because you have decided to leave, you may begin dreaming of the great new position you'll soon find and start to let up at your current job. Wrong. You must continue to work as hard as ever. You still owe your company good work, and when the time comes, it will be critical to leave on a high note with a great reputation. And letting up is a sure indication that a person is seeking greener pastures.

You may even be tempted to quit altogether. Don't. Recruiters and ultimately employers prefer to hire people who are currently working. If you have been laid off, that's not your fault, but you can help your cause by staying "employed" as a writer, speaker, consultant or volunteer.

Most importantly, if you keep working, you are still earning an income, which buys you time to find the right job for you and not the first thing that comes along. This is extremely important; you don't want to jump from the frying pan into the fire. It could be months before you find the right job. Better to wait and continue working while you search.

No Surprise—It's Hard Work

You must also be willing—and prepared—to devote time and energy to your job search: paperwork, interviews, phone calls, e-mails. If you are employed, these things must all be done either privately on your own time at work, or at home after hours. If you currently have no job, then you must make your search your full-time job—you'll have to sacrifice a golf game or two. Forget what the commercials say; you can't just zip out your resume to some Web sites, and voila, the perfect job appears. The process takes time and patience. But be careful not to get discouraged or overwhelmed. Spend time with family and friends, get proper exercise and rest. You will find what you're looking for.

Look at Yourself in the Mirror

If you ask any professional, chances are they can tell you the most minute details of their product or service: what it has to offer, why it's better than the competition.

But ask the same person to name the details of their own career accomplishments, or better yet, their real career desires, and many a professional is left perplexed—not because they haven't been successful, but because they simply haven't given it enough thought. Sure, they type up their major achievements once a year for a review, but they focus so much on the company's numbers and goals that they forget to analyze what they have done as a whole. They overlook their other accomplishments that could lead to a new and better position. Beyond accomplishments, they overlook their own experiences, expertise, and personal growth. They often have a narrow view of who they are and what they've done, shaped by specific tasks done in their job. What's needed is the bigger picture, not just the details. The point: how can you present a good picture of yourself to a company or a recruiter if you don't even know, or realize, all you can do?

Developing Your Personal Profile:
Business Accomplishments

In a job search, you are the product. You need to understand yourself as a product–a product with features. The better you "take inventory" and know yourself and your past, present and future capabilities, the better you can sell yourself to a company or a recruiter. This is a self-assessment–but don't forget to include the perceptions of others, inside and outside your company, in your "inventory." And it isn't just about you or your career persona.You also want to inventory your goals, desires and needs from a job. Establishing these now will save you from going in the wrong career direction later.

Don't worry about a resume yet. Get a pen and paper and think "big picture." First consider the quantifiable accomplishments you have. These are the obvious accomplishments that probably exist on your current resume: specific goals you have reached in past jobs, actual percentages and dollar amounts you have improved in your tenure, ideas and products you have launched or helped launched. Think in the bigger picture–projects and ideas you have created or managed. Think of all contributions to your current organization. Think of contributions outside your organization–trade show appearances and talks, publications, maybe a patentable idea or two? Write them down. Ideally you have kept copies of past annual reviews and other documents that praise you–articles, memos, e-mails and the like. Be sure to consult these for other areas in which you have shone over the years in your current and previous jobs.

Consider your soft skills. These are achievements that are less obvious but just as important in running a business: managing and leading younger staffers, volunteering for committees and projects in other areas of the company, articles you've written for trade journals, speeches given at conferences. Yet many of us don't include them on our resumes because we don't think of them as important. But it may be these very things that set you apart from the others.

If you volunteer outside of work, add that as well, especially if you serve on the board of a charity. You may also want to list personal or athletic accomplishments, such as running a marathon or sailing in races. These show determination and persistence.

Developing Your Personal Profile: Personal Characteristics

Now think again about you. This time as a person, not an employee. What personality traits have made you good at what you do? What traits about yourself are you particularly proud of? Are you cheerful and easygoing? Confident and determined? A good leader? What traits do you dislike?

Now look again at your past reviews and see what negative feedback you have received. Do you see any patterns? Have your problems been job-specific or are they more personality-related? Are they issues you have repeatedly struggled with because you are not on the right career path? What can you do to improve upon them?

Also consider what you like and don't like about working, both in your current job and those past. What frustrates you—not just about your company but also about working in general? Do you like advising those beneath you, or would you rather have less of a mentor role? Are you a "big picture" person or a detail person, or are you versatile enough to deal in both worlds? Do you become bogged down or frustrated with minor management of details to the detriment of getting the job done? Maybe you are a people person, but find that you don't interact with them enough in your line of work. Do you prefer preparing a presentation as opposed to giving it? Are you an idea person, but cannot manage to communicate your thoughts into words very well? What kind of job might allow you to be a better, happier employee?

Outside Help

If you want more insight as to why you are the way you are and how you could use it to your advantage in your career, there are a number of outside sources that can help you.

Hundreds of books and Web sites are available on meshing careers with personality traits. For example, there is the Myers-Briggs test, in which you answer a series of questions and are ultimately measured in terms of communication style and thought process. This test exists in a condensed form on various sites (although keep in mind you should use the results only as a guideline, not as hard fact). If you want to try a new field altogether there are lots of specific publications and career Web sites to help you.

Career Counselors

If you still need assistance, you might consider contacting a professional career counselor. Career counselors assist people in reconciling their career desires with their personal desires and traits. Career counselors generally have a background in psychology and/or business, a certification in career counseling, and aim to help you become a better, happier person in a work field you enjoy. You should not be embarrassed for needing a career counselor.

Career counselors typically are not recruiters–and vice versa–though some may have experience in both fields. However, if a career counselor (or a recruiter for that matter) guarantees that you will find a job by using his or her services, or makes you sign contracts and pay fees up-front, you do not want to hire them. No one can guarantee to find you a job.

In searching for a counselor, you may also find a number of listings for "career coaches," "executive coaches," and "life coaches." These are also good possibilities to help in your career assessment. The difference between coaches and career counselors is usually a specialized degree or certification. Coaches aren't certified but are often former executives who can understand your situation since they have been in the trenches. Again, be wary of guarantees or payments demanded upfront. For more information on finding a good career counselor in your area, check the National Board of Certified Counselors Web site at www.nbcc.org. Again, remember, career counselors and coaches won't get you a job, but will help you better prepare to get a job and to work more effectively with an executive recruiter.

FINDING YOUR DREAM JOB

As hinted earlier, the assessment doesn't stop with a picture of you, standing all by yourself. The better, more useful, more appealing picture is of you, with a background, in a job. It is important to think through what works for you and develop a profile of the background—the position or types of positions that suit you best.

Profiling Your New Job

Ask yourself what you want in a job. Be direct with the question and be direct with the answer. And don't be afraid to list details. Understand both the big picture and the details. The details can make the difference between a terrific job and a terrible one. Hours worked, travel, number and kinds of people you work with, the personality and flexibility of the company. There's a longer list below. This inventory may sound a bit pedantic, but you'd be surprised how often it gets overlooked. People get caught up in the assumption that the grass is greener on the other side of the fence. They don't look at the details, then they find out that it really isn't greener at all.

A Position Blueprint

First ask yourself what you have liked and disliked about your current and past jobs? Questions like:

- Do you wish to stay in the same field or try something new?
- Do you like to work individually or in teams?
- Do you thrive in a structured or an unstructured environment?
- Do you like to focus on one task or multitask in a job?
- Are you happy with a more established work atmosphere, or might you like to attempt something riskier, like a dot-com startup?
- Do you prefer traditional work hours and attire, or would you be happier in a more laid-back environment?
- Do you thrive in larger or smaller organizations?
- What industry or specialties work best for you?

Be honest and don't hold back. Picture your perfect job and list its characteristics. The better the idea you have now, the more you can give a recruiter to help match you. Form a concrete idea in your mind now of what you want, and you'll be less likely to settle for something down the road. A good exercise: with these characteristics in mind, lay out your own personal characteristics and decide if you're a good fit–why and why not. Practice explaining why you're a fit. This "practice" will help you work with recruiters and interview for the positions.

Profiling Your Dream Company

Companies have reputations, some more obvious than others. We all experience many companies as customers. You can get a good "flavor" for Starbucks just by walking in the door. With others, it's a little more difficult. All publicly traded and many private companies publish information in the form of annual reports. Most have Web sites and other forms of marketing and public relations "collateral." Still, it is sometimes hard to get the real skinny–what it's like to work there, what the people are like, how employees are treated, what pay and benefits are available. And, in most cases, it isn't just the company that's important–it's the industry. The retail industry environment is simply different than the investment banking environment.

Getting this "real life" picture sometimes takes a little detective work. It's great to talk to employees if that's possible. Talk to companies in the supply chain. If you want to learn more about the computer industry, talk to retailers that sell computers. It's a good idea to follow press releases and journalistic commentary about companies in business journals or portals such as Yahoo!Finance news. For a more pithy, opinionated commentary, you can look at the company "chat" boards inside Yahoo!Finance. You may have to cover your eyes at times, but company employees bare their souls about their issues, their problems, their managers all the time.

For More Inside Scoop

To get more of an insider's view of a company, Web sites like Wetfeet.com provide a company's basic information and, for a fee, a more detailed snapshot of how a company is faring. You can also visit the somewhat renegade, yet nonetheless from-the-horse's-mouth layoff listing sites. Their language is rough, and they have a rumor mill aspect, but if you want the nitty gritty on how a company is doing and whether it plans layoffs or mergers, these are the sites that will post that information first (much to their companies' dismay).

Specialized sites also help with relocation decisions. Perhaps you know you want to relocate with your next job, but don't know what your target city is like. You can research cost of living, salaries, mortgages, crime rates, and schools on the Web at sites like Salary.com and Homefair.com.

The Resume

While it's human nature for people to enjoy talking about themselves, few tasks are more grueling than preparing one's resume. This exercise will be examined in detail in Chapter 8. But, you may already have much of the required material; you just need to format it accordingly.

For insight, you can research executive resume examples in books or on the Web. They usually fall into two camps: chronological (the most common, it groups skills by the most recent job) and functional (groups jobs according to skills). You'll need to research which format is best for your desired line of work, as executive, technical, and creative resumes have subtle differences. If you are changing fields, the new field may require a different type of resume format from what you have used in the past. There are also new trends that might apply to you if you have not conducted a job search in some time. For example, computer skills are a must-have on any resume, regardless of whether your career is technical or not. Again, Chapter 8 will cover the details of structure, content, tone and manner for executive resumes.

While you can write a solid resume yourself, at this time you may want to consider having a professional resume writer (designation CPRW) help you. Often these experts are also career counselors and/or coaches. This is not only acceptable. It can help you kill two birds with one stone.

JOB-SEARCH OPTIONS

Now that you know what you have to offer and the kind of job you desire, you can officially begin your search. You have many options; if you have not done a job search in some time, the number may surprise you. Some are better than others, and you may want to use all the methods concurrently.

Executive Recruiters

Obviously you are considering working with an executive recruiter or you wouldn't be reading this book! Once you reach a certain level in your career, a recruiter may be the single best way not only to find a new position but also to help you negotiate the best possible package. But you don't have to be a six-figure executive to benefit from a recruiter.

As further discussed in Chapter 3, recruiting firms fall into two camps—contingency and retained. A contingency firm's payment is contingent on whether or not the firm fills a position for the client company. The recruiters are not paid until a placement is made. For that reason, recruiters from contingency firms may work a little harder to get you that interview or to help present you for a search that may not be your exact fit, but that you believe could hold potential anyway. Although contingency firms mainly work with mid- to senior-level management jobs, they place people at salary levels ranging from $18K to $100K. If you are a mid-level working professional, you're more likely to be working with a contingency firm.

Recruiters with retained firms work with higher-level companies and executive jobs, and fewer of them—sometimes as few as two or three a year. They are paid with an upfront retainer by the client company, regardless of whether a candidate is hired. You won't need to call a retained firm; they will contact you if a position arises that could fit you. A retained firm is looking for an exact match to what a company has requested and, unlike contingency firms, will not cast as wide a net.

You may have worked with a recruiter before, have recently been contacted by one, or are considering contacting one yourself. However you meet them, use them! Working with a recruiter sometimes requires building a relationship in advance of your job search. You should never avoid

23

The Executive Recruiter Search Process. The task of identifying and appraising well-qualified executives is painstaking and time consuming and must be governed by an orderly approach, consisting of major steps or phases, if it is to be successful. These steps represent the broad phases of a typical search assignment and identify major areas of activity involved in the work that recruiters do for clients.

These steps are interrelated and interdependent, but they are often adapted and modified by search consultants as they work out their own approaches to client engagements. The professional search process does not depend on luck, shortcuts or gimmicks, but on a step-by-step procedure whereby a list of potentially suitable executives is reduced to several uniquely qualified candidates. The aim is not merely to produce qualified candidates (which is relatively easy) but the very best candidates available.

recruiters even if you're not currently looking. Building the relationship—even by just helping them locate other candidates—is likely to pay dividends for you some day.

Networking

Nothing beats networking. Eighty percent of jobs are found this way because networking gives you an "in," someone who, directly or indirectly, can vouch for you, as opposed to blindly applying to a want-ad. Patience is needed, however, as networking may not put you in touch with the perfect job so much as a friend of the secretary of the hiring manager. Still, it's a leg up, and the best part is you can network anywhere—on an airplane, at conferences, at the gym.

Professional Organizations

Not only do member organizations give you a chance to shine by writing articles for their publications or speaking at engagements, but they have their own job boards and Web sites. The downside is they have dues, they might meet infrequently, and other people will vie for the same jobs you see. Still, they are a must for furthering your career and seeing what kinds of positions are available.

Trade Journals and Business Journals

Financial Times, The Wall Street Journal, Investors Business Daily. Much like professional organizations, these publications get you elbowing with people in the same business and keep you up to date on the latest news and trends. However, you are also learning this information at the same time as other potential job seekers in your industry. They are great for informing you on the types of jobs available in your industry, but don't rely on them for finding one.

Your local newspaper can also provide you with information and job listings. While most newspaper want-ads are still essentially for blue collar or lower-level professional jobs, it is still worth looking into your local newspaper's ads, especially if you are in a major market. Because many major papers have partnered with national job Web sites to "power" their job sections, they do have higher-level jobs as well. Still, don't hold your breath waiting to get the job.

Job Boards and Job Web Sites

Like newspapers, job boards and Web sites can be a great way to see what types of positions are available in your industry. Used interchangeably, job boards are Web sites that usually list jobs only. Job Web sites tend to have jobs and supplemental information, like articles and tools to help you brush up on your interviewing skills and cover letter tips.

The largest job boards/sites (Monster, HotJobs, Careerbuilder, Yahoo!) have thousands of jobs you can search for free (it's the companies that pay to have their jobs posted there). While the sign-up process can be grueling, you can store your resumes and cover letters to use over and over again. You can set up "search agents" to e-mail you with jobs that match your qualifications. And the jobs range from minimum wage to freelance to high-level executive positions.

However, there are many downsides to using these sites. For one, sometimes the positions remain "open" (they remain on the site indefinitely) as a way for companies to stock their resume databases from year-round applications. The position—if it ever existed in the first place—may even be filled, but the posting remains. Great for the company, but not so good for you.

Also, many of the higher-level positions will be posted anonymously. There will be a general job description, but the company name is not mentioned. This is risky if your job-search privacy is a must.

Competition is fierce with job boards, as people from all over the country will apply. And while storing your resume is convenient (these sites usually do not allow you to send attachments), you must take care to enter information perfectly, or formatting issues (strange characters and line breaks) can occur once you hit "send."

You might want to bypass the middleman and go directly to Web sites of specific companies you would like to work for. Most companies now have their available jobs listed online, along with the application process. Again, there is competition, but it's not as extreme as that of the national job boards (unless the job you want is also listed on a national job site). But you can usually send in your resume as an attachment (thus, no formatting mistakes), and you can often find an actual person's name–someone you may contact again in the future. But be aware that many a posting company really intends to hire internally.

As you use the Web, you'll soon become aware of another downside: lack of dialog and acknowledgment. The Web is a great tool, but it automates and depersonalizes communication to the point where you can't expect an acknowledgment–even for receipt of your materials. The sheer volume of communication usually precludes personal response, even to e-mails. You will have to learn to accept no answer or no response, and not to take it personally.

WORKING WITH AN EXECUTIVE RECRUITER

As this book is about working with executive recruiters, it's now time to focus on that topic.

Why Work with a Recruiter?

With so many other job-search options, you may ask yourself why use a recruiter in the first place? After all, for mid-level jobs, only some 10 to 15 percent of job-search candidates find jobs through recruiters. But there are so many benefits to using a recruiter, that if you are one of that 15 percent, you'll likely have the job you want and for the pay you want as well. The question often becomes not "why use a recruiter" but "why not?" Here are some reasons for using a recruiter:

- Recruiters know the hidden job market. Many, if not most, of the jobs they have won't be found in the want-ads, nor anywhere else.
- A job found with a recruiter will be secure. If a company is willing to take the time and expense to use a recruiter, the person they are hiring is one they will want to keep.
- A recruiter can sell you. Recruiters can help you "play above your resume." They have met you and can play up your advantages to a potential employer. They can also help coach you with context and tips specific to that company.
- Recruiters will help you achieve compensation goals. Recruiter fees are based on the salary package you receive. Therefore, they will be more likely to "push" for you in negotiations. And if negotiating is something you are uncomfortable with, a recruiter can relieve you of that burden.
- And the hiring company pays. Best of all, the entire process is free to you–100 percent free.

Getting Started

You probably already know how to do the other job search methods we have mentioned–networking, searching on Web sites. But working with a recruiter may be less familiar. How do you begin a relationship with a recruiter?

The first step is not to wait until you are laid off or desperate for a new job. The best time to contact a recruiter (or entertain their contact of you) is when you are employed and even happy at your job. If you are desperate now, don't panic. Just get going, and be sure to give yourself the proper time to get through the recruitment process (usually three to four months at least) as you carefully evaluate the jobs that come your way.

You need to locate the right firm. This is a group that has a good track record, has good references and recommendations, and is generally friendly and professional. It does not require any payment from you, and if it does, move on immediately. You can locate good firms by asking professional contacts or attending conferences and job fairs. You can also improve your chances of being contacted by a firm by raising your own image in your field—speaking at events, volunteering, visiting trade events, writing articles. Like baseball scouts, if you're good, they're watching. See Chapters 5 and 6 for more on building a relationship with a recruiter.

Whether the firm calls you or you call it, you'll next undergo several telephone interviews in which you will give an overall picture of your work history and why you would like to change. You need to have ready your updated resume and a list of ideal companies and/or job situations. (Be sure to keep your resume updated from now on!) Also, do be candid about your current salary and benefits when asked—the recruiter needs to know this information. Don't be afraid to ask questions about the potential position, but don't be surprised if the recruiter doesn't disclose all of the information; you are merely in the preliminary stages of a job hunt. More about this aspect of the recruiter relationship is brought to light in Chapter 7.

If you continue to qualify, you will be given an in-person interview, first with the recruiter and then with the company. If you are offered the job, the recruiter will work with you on your references and negotiation.

At any point in this process, you may find that the job is not right for you (or you are not right for the job). Do not worry. It's all about the relationship. You can help provide the recruiter with other candidates for other searches they are conducting. And chances are if you performed well in this search, there will likely be another one very soon, and that one just might work out. Once you do find a position, you'll want to continue your relationship with your recruiter. He or she will appreciate other referrals you can give, and the closer you stay to "top of mind," the faster they will call you the next time another potential position becomes open.

For Senior Executives Only

Because most professionals fall somewhere into the $30K-$100K salary range, and because contingency firms outnumber retained firms about two to one, much of the advice we'll give in this book pertains to the average professional. But for those who have reached a certain level in their career

Five Easy Pieces of Advice on Dealing with Executive Recruiters

1. Start relating to recruiters in your field long before you need them or they call you.

2. Check them out if you've never heard of them.

3. Never lie or even stretch the truth about education, job experience, salary, etc.

4. Level with the recruiter if you'd entertain a counteroffer to stay.

SOURCE: James H. Kennedy, founder and former editor of *Executive Recruiter News*

(well over $100K, title of CEO, VP or similar), some of the advice about job search and working with recruiters applies differently. First, you will most likely be working with a recruiter. According to a Coopers & Lybrand survey, 64 percent of all executive-level job placements are done by executive recruiters. That recruiter is most likely to be a retained search recruiter. Retained search professionals are well-known in their industries (or even to the general public) and considered authorities in their lines of business. Thus, a recruiter with a known firm will likely contact you first. There is no need for a senior executive to send out resumes. Retained firms rarely, if ever, use them. The negotiation process is more important. There are other perks besides salary–company cars, club memberships, bonuses and stock options. Executives will also want to ask more questions about the company: When were bonuses last paid out? How well does the executive board get along? Finally, you will also need to consider aspects of this level of responsibility that other professionals have not achieved yet: What does this move mean for your image? Could this job mean further accomplishments like book deals and television? What will be the publicity impact on your career? An executive recruiter will not only help an executive receive the best job, but can also assist in navigating the finer points of an all-around job package.

PART 2
ABOUT
RECRUITING
FIRMS

CHAPTER 3
UNDERSTANDING EXECUTIVE RECRUITERS

Respect the recruiter's time–and also yours. Chatting for
the sake of chatting doesn't help you or the placement
manager–both of you should be busy. I'm not suggesting
that you don't talk with each other–just make it short.
– Max Messmer, CEO, Robert Half International

s you enter the job market, you realize the task at hand is to market you–your skills, background, personality and value–as a product. You must market that product to a customer–in this case, an employer. You must execute with near perfection, for you know the employer is a very discerning customer–a customer able (and willing) to select the next product on the shelf at the slightest sign of imperfection.

As with most tasks in business and life, there are alternative paths to getting the job search done. You can do it yourself, have others do it for you, or a combination of the two. Perhaps you do your own taxes, remodel your own house, fix your own car, and manage your own investments. You do it yourself with the idea of saving money and gaining the satisfaction of doing it with your own hands. You're willing to accept the risk of slightly-less-than-professional grade work. You're willing to devote the time it takes to get it done. You trade off a little time and quality to save money and build pride of ownership.

WORKING WITH JOB-SEARCH PROFESSIONALS

But the question of whether or not to take on these tasks nags even the most devoted do-it-yourselfer. Is it better to leave such an important task in the hands of a professional who has the experience, knowledge, time, information, resources and focus to get it done right? With professional quality and speed? That sounds pretty good—get the pros to work for you, sleep better at night and use your valuable time for something else. Yes, but what about the cost?

You apply this line of thinking to your upcoming job search. Should you do it yourself or engage a professional? Sure, there's the Internet, your friends, and the word-of-mouth network. There is a vast array of newspapers, publications, and other resources at your disposal to build a job-search campaign. After all, you're a professional yourself and can apply your own professional skills to managing the search, so why not give it a try?

Time to evaluate. Just like your home deck project or stock picks, you can do this yourself. And you may be good at it. However, using professionals in a job search offers many of the same benefits afforded to other professional engagements—skill, experience, time, resources, information and focus. Finding people for jobs is a professional recruiter's business, and you're trying to find a job. They have inside information on the positions and job market that you likely will never have, and most have the skills to connect you to those positions quickly and effectively.

And perhaps the best part: there is no cost to you. The professional services of a recruiter are paid by the employer. So you can get the professional touch at no cost. Is it compelling to broaden your reach to other job possibilities and perfect your job campaign at no cost? The answer—especially for high-level professionals to whom information, time and focus are particularly important—may well be yes.

But there is a catch, albeit a small one. In most situations, when you engage with a professional, you hire them, pay them and tell them what to do. With executive recruiters, it's different—they are hired and paid for by the employers. Their "product" is to deliver you to the employer—not to deliver the employer to you. So using a professional when you're not the direct customer is a slightly different game. Most of the advantages apply, but you don't command the attention nor have the control normally afforded to a true customer.

Understanding the Process

As in most other endeavors, before you entrust a vital part of your life or business to a professional, you want to understand who they are and what they do. You want to understand their business and their reputation. You want to know how to work with them. You want to know what you will have to do to assure a successful result. Like other professional engagements, working with an executive recruiter requires a good deal of cooperation from you.

THE EXECUTIVE RECRUITING INDUSTRY

This chapter and those that follow are designed to give you an understanding of the recruiting industry and how you should work with it as a position seeker. In particular, this chapter explains what an executive recruiter is and provides an overview of the executive recruiting industry. Chapter 4 explores how executive recruiters operate. Chapters 5 through 8 explain how you should work with an executive recruiter to best achieve your objectives. From these discussions you should take away who the professionals are, what they do, and how they do it. From that, you can make informed decisions on whether or not to engage a recruiter—and, if so, which firm to engage. And you'll learn how to work with the recruiter to land the best job with the least amount of time and wasted effort.

Executive recruiting as a profession emerged during World War II, where employable people were scarce, and the need for employees, particularly in specialized fields, was great. Firms faced a daunting task in finding the right people. Recognizing this need, recruiting firms sprang up at all levels to help get it done. Some recruiters—primarily retained search firms—evolved from the management consulting industry. Over the years, increasing job specialization and job and geographic mobility have not only sustained the recruiting industry but have caused it to evolve, expand and specialize to arrive where it is today.

What Is an Executive Recruiter?

There are several important concepts within this definition as follows:

■ **Recruiter.** A recruiter in this case is an individual or firm that specializes in the field of recruiting. For this purpose the firm is a separate entity from the client firm wishing to hire someone. Thus, recruiting done by a company's own HR organization is not considered executive recruiting.

■ **Executive.** The term "executive" can have broad or narrow meaning depending on whom you talk to. Generally speaking, for the purpose of identifying executive recruiting, the term means a professional position–often but not always managerial. Key "individual contributor" positions in both managerial and technical professions–for instance, market researchers, design engineers, or microbiologists–can also be acquired through executive recruiters. Although it varies somewhat by industry, region, profession, and type of recruiter, the positions involved typically have salaries in excess of $50K/year.

Executive Recruiter.

An executive recruiter is a professional firm or individual who, for a fee, helps their client organizations identify, evaluate, and hire skilled individuals qualified to fill specific positions in industry, government and the non-profit sector.

■ **Fee.** Obviously any professional service is rendered for a fee. At one time, services that would be described today as executive recruiting were sometimes paid for by the employee. The predictable result: only the "desperate" employee was willing to pay the fee to get help. Thus hiring companies didn't get access to the best candidates. Poor matches were the result. Many years ago the industry transitioned to the fee paid model, where the employer pays the fee to the recruiter. The fee is typically a percentage of the first year's salary of the employee, an hourly or daily rate, or a combination, depending on the type of recruiter and services provided. Be very clear that you, as job seeker, should never pay this fee nor any portion of it. If so, you're not dealing with a credible professional executive recruiter.

■ **Client.** Predictably, it is the hiring company, because it is paying the fee. This is one of the most important concepts in understanding executive recruiters. The executive recruiter is not–emphatically not–working for you, the job seeker. The recruiter is working with the employer firm to identify and place the best candidate to meet the employer's need. The employer firm is the customer; you are part of the product. The recruiter's job is to find people for positions, not positions for people. What does that mean? While the recruiter will build a respectful relationship with you to accomplish their task, you shouldn't expect to be treated as the customer.

- **Skilled individuals.** As stated earlier, executive recruiters are brought in to find people with specific skills–usually professional, managerial or technical–for specific positions. Executive recruiters normally don't hire for hourly or "rank and file" positions. You, as a skilled individual may be referred to as the job seeker or candidate, but never as the client or customer.

- **Specific positions.** Specific positions are known, open–or soon to be open–positions in a firm. These searches are usually to replace a key officer or manager or to grow or start a new business. Executive recruiters are not employed just to capture file resumes to have on hand for the next opening. Recruiters recruit for an open position with a defined job description. Occasionally, the recruiter may get involved as a consultant in defining the position description or the compensation associated with it.

What is a "Headhunter"?

"Headhunter" is a pejorative but popular term used to describe an executive recruiter, especially one who works on contingency. It has stuck over the years, and at one time reflected some of the aggressive and predatory practices employed by fringe players in the industry. While not a favorite of industry professionals, the term "headhunter" does get a lot of use in informal conversation.

What Is an "Executive Search Consultant"?

The term "executive search consultant" may be applied to any executive recruiter but more commonly refers to the "retained" recruiter. These recruiters are engaged not only for search but also other consulting services around developing the job position and job description. These retained recruiters are paid like a consultant, collecting fees whether an employee is hired or not. A more complete description of "retained" and "contingency" recruiters follows shortly.

What an Executive Recruiter Isn't

Sometimes the best way to understand something is to understand what it isn't:

■ An executive recruiter is not a company's human resources (HR) or employment department. Companies may engage searches of their own, occasionally employing many of the same techniques as the professional recruiter. But for many reasons described further in Chapter 4, most companies prefer to engage professionals–particularly for sensitive high-level management positions. Most companies don't have the bandwidth or information to conduct extensive executive searches.

■ An executive recruiter is not an employment agency. Employment agencies find jobs for people, not people for jobs. Typically they aim at the lower end, rank-and-file part of the workforce, and many specialize in temporary assignments.

Industry Snapshot

Understanding a business means understanding not only its product but its players–how many, how big, and who the leaders are.

There are about 5,700 executive recruiting firms operating over 8,100 office locations in the United States. Among this group are many firms with only one office and perhaps only one individual providing the service. At the other end of the scale is Management Recruiters International (MRI) with over 400 locations in the U.S. There are about 50,000 professionals employed in the executive recruiting industry.

Executive recruiters are concentrated in centers of industry and commerce, mainly on the East and West Coasts and selected major metropolitan locations elsewhere. There are 300 recruiting firm offices in New York City, while there are only three in all of North Dakota. Most firms operate nationwide.

According to *Executive Recuiters News,* published by Kennedy Information, Inc., the top 10 retained recruiting firms in the U.S., based on 2001 U.S. retained search revenues are:

■ Heidrick & Struggles International
■ Korn/Ferry International
■ Spencer Stuart
■ Russell Reynolds Associates
■ TMP Worldwide Executive Search

- Egon Zehnder International
- DHR International
- Christian & Timbers
- Ray and Berndtson
- Witt/Kieffer, Ford, Hadelman and Lloyd

The average billing per individual recruiting consultant runs upward of $1 million per year at the large firms and approaches $2 million in good years.

Growth and Business Cycle

The executive recruiting industry has been growing steadily over the years, as industry and job changes have become more frequent and geography becomes less of a barrier. Predictably, executive recruiting business activity is greater during boom times. Client companies are growing and hiring, while the labor market is tighter and good recruits are harder to find, which makes recruiter services even more important. Twenty to 40 percent swings in recruiting volume from year to year are not uncommon.

TYPES OF EXECUTIVE RECRUITERS

With most professions, as demand grows and needs become more complex, they tend to specialize. This is certainly the case in medicine, law, public accounting, and most other large professional fields. Niches grow big enough to become viable markets. Different business models also evolve, as they have in medicine (private practice, HMO, PPO, etc).

Clearly this phenomenon has occurred in the executive recruiting profession. There are two major business models, or types of executive recruiters–retainer and contingency. Each type has a very different operating model and operates in different parts of the executive recruiting market, albeit with some overlap. Further, many recruiters choose to specialize only in certain professions, industries, or geographies. As specialists, they become experts in a particular field or industry and thus operate more effectively. Others maintain a more generalist model, applying their process to a broad range of clients. Note that the classifications work together:

there are generalists and specialists operating as retainer firms, and generalists and specialists operating as contingency firms.

The Boutique Down the Street

There has been a trend towards specialist, or boutique, firms that focus on one type of function or industry or a narrow combination of these. As an example, Kelly & Company in New York finds HR professionals specifically for HR consulting firms. Jones-Parker/Starr in North Carolina recruits recruiters for retained search firms. And many recruiters have specialized at the top end of the "food chain," searching only for CEO or VP positions with a minimum salary of $200K plus. Some may do only a handful of searches each year. These boutique specialists thoroughly know the business they serve, their clients and all of their potential candidates. They sell their expertise and their network.

The rest of this chapter explains the difference between retainer and contingency firms and further describes the specialization in the recruiting industry.

RETAINER AND CONTINGENCY FIRMS

Retainer and contingency recruiters operate with very different business models. As a result, your expectations and working relationship with them will be quite different. It is extremely important to understand these models and their differences, and to identify the type of recruiter when working with them. There are 1,700 retained search firms and 3,900 contingency firms in the U.S.

Retained Search Firms

A retainer, or retained, search firm is hired by the client company for a specified period of time to find a key candidate to fill a position. A retainer is paid regardless of the results of the search. The agreement is exclusive–that is, it is the only firm involved in the search at a given time. In most scenarios it operates at the upper ranges of the corporate ladder, working to fill senior executive or key employee positions paying $100K annually or more. It may even recruit corporate board members. It may be involved in a consulting role for position design, compensation, or other personnel/HR consulting issues. Its goal is to satisfy the client by getting the best candidate hired. As a result, the screening process is very selective, and it will bring only a few highly qualified candidates to the client. Remember—a retainer firm gets paid regardless of hire, so why not find the best recruit for the next assignment?

Working with a retained search firm, as a job seeker, can be tricky. First of all, they will only want to know about you if you're a highly qualified, "high-end" candidate. They don't have to place a candidate to earn their fee, so if you're not the right candidate, there is no incentive to try to move you into the position. If they need you, they will find you—they generally don't keep large files of resumes from job seekers, and it is generally harder to get them interested in you. But the flip side: if you are contacted by a retained search firm, you are likely on a short list of candidates. Finally, the nature of the engagement is exclusive—if a retained recruiter contacts you, you cannot be contacted by any other recruiter at that firm. If retained by the company with which you're currently employed, you are "off limits" for any other position the search firm may have. So with retained firms, any exposure you get as a job seeker is likely to be quality exposure, but you may be exposed to only a handful of positions. And it's difficult to get onto their radar screen.

Contingency Firms

Contingency firms operate at the less senior levels of management and the executive recruiting landscape. Most recruiters are contingency, and most placements use the contingency model. The contingency firm gets paid only when a candidate is hired. This is the key difference when compared to retained firms. So the efforts of a contingency firm go unrewarded unless someone is placed. Result? The contingency firm brings as many candidates to the table as the employer will accept, hoping to land the successful one. The fit between the candidate and position may not be as good, as the contingency firm is motivated to sell a candidate for hire even if not perfectly qualified. It acts as quickly as possible to beat the competition and move on to the next assignment. Contingency engagements are not exclusive, so it becomes a bit of a contest to obtain placement ahead of the competition. Contingency firms are more motivated to give more advice and help to the candidate, for that usually results in a faster placement (and payment for the recruiter).

Contingency firms mainly operate at the middle levels of management and with skilled individual contributors, such as engineers and IT professionals. They tend to operate more in high turnover industries and job functions, such as retail, healthcare, and some areas of technology. Some go to lower-tier nonprofessionals, such as office and service workers. Although some positions exceed $100K annually, most lie in the $50K - $100K range and can go as low as $30K. In recent years, the contingency and retained models (and recruiters) have tended to blend, with retained firms accepting contingency assignments and contingency firms providing some of the client services of a retained firm, and reaching higher into the management ranks.

Contingency firms are more the true "matchmakers" in the recruiting industry. They will match many job seekers to many positions. Contingency firms will give you more exposure. They need as many qualified candidates as possible in their database to meet client needs quickly. But there is no such thing as a short list–your name is likely to be circulated with many others. The probability of match to any given job is reduced. If you are early in your career, wish to cast a wide net, and aren't worried about your company discovering your search, contingency firms can be the right choice.

SPECIALISTS AND GENERALISTS

Most executive recruiters specialize in specific industries and kinds of jobs. In doing so they develop efficiency and reputation, which in turn leads to more of the same. Some recruiters will act as generalists but also maintain certain specialties.

Recruiters specialize in two dimensions: industry and job function. Kennedy Information uses a proprietary classification system in its executive recruiter database and *The Directory of Executive Recruiters*. See Appendix for a complete listing of industry and job function classifications.

TABLE: Retainer and Contingency Firms Compared.

	RETAINER	CONTINGENCY
Number of firms	1,700	3,900
Largest firm in U.S.	Heidrick & Struggles International	Management Recruiters International (MRI)
How paid	Engaged as consultants	Paid upon hire
Types of positions	Senior executive, management, technical specialist	Mid-level managers, professionals, high-turnover industries
Position salary range	$100K +	$30K - $100K
Exclusivity: firms per position	One firm	Can be many firms
Approach	Not in business to get you a job	Wants to get you hired
Job-seeker exposure	Limited but high quality, thorough	Wider but brief exposure to each hiring firm
Job seeker accessibility	Difficult	Relatively easy
Job seeker courtesy	Usually very good once noticed	Varies–typically more helpful to candidate
How they connect with job seeker	Network, highly targeted phone calls, online research	Advertisements, resume files, some phone calls, online research, networking
Other services	Position and compensation consulting	Usually none

Industries

There are 21 different industries, plus generalist and non-classifiable. The 21 general classifications include such industries as Construction, Manufacturing, Finance, Hospitality, Media and Communications. Within each general classification there may be as many as 30 subclassifications (there are 65 subclassifications in total). So for instance, Media has four subclassifications: Advertising, Publishing, New Media, and Broadcast/Film.

Job Functions

There are 11 major job function classifications and (also) 65 sub-classifications within the 11 major classes. For example, the major class Sales & Marketing has within it:

- Advertising, Sales Promotion
- Marketing & Product Research
- Marketing Management
- Sales and Sales Management
- Direct Mail, Marketing, Telemarketing
- Customer Service
- Public Relations

So if you want to look for a job as a marketing manager within the broadcast industry, it is easy to identify recruiters working in that specialty within that industry.

Keyword Specialties

A less formal but very interesting classification, particularly for the candidate with very specific skills or interests, is the Kennedy Recruiter Specialties Index. Found in the Kennedy *Directory of Executive Recruiters*, the keyword specialties list allows you to pinpoint firms dealing in very specialized fields, such as Biostatistics E-business, or SAP. There are about 500 of these specialties identified. Not only are the categories specific, but so are the recruiters—instead of firms, the index identifies individual recruiters within the firms handling the specialty. So if you're looking for a position in the field of neural networks, cut to the chase and contact Urania Van Applebaum at Engineering Solutions International.

This chapter provides an overview of the executive search industry and its firms. Additional detail can be found in the Appendices, in the Kennedy Guide to Executive Recruiters, and on the Kennedy Information Web site (www.kennedyinfo.com). With this foundation in mind, Chapter 4 explains how executive recruiters operate, how they engage with clients, and how they engage with you.

Anatomy of an Executive Recruiter

According to executive recruiter William R. Wilkinson, of Wilkinson and Ives, San Francisco, the following is a profile of the typical headhunter:

Your typical headhunter looks mostly like you and me, provided you are a male WASP between thirty-five and sixty and you identify with the executive public at large. Some recruiters are tall, well-dressed, debonair and polished "tennis anyone?" types; others are short and round with food spots on their ties and pants badly in need of pressing. A few appear to be fast-talking city slickers, and maybe are. Others are slower moving clod-kicker types who punctuate their questions and comments with hesitation and who like to laugh a lot. Most are happily married family men who mow their own lawns on Saturdays and shoot an occasional 113 at their country clubs. About a third have been divorced and remarried. Almost all aspire to have their children graduate from good colleges and marry talented mates.

The more successful ones have a great deal in common: They are intellectually bright, socially adept, sensitive and quick in forming good judgments about [person]-job matches or mismatches, and they know either in person or over the telephone just about everybody they need to know to conduct their business well.

Generally, all of them can be found, when at work, garbed in at least one article of Brooks Brothers clothing. Their backgrounds are varied. Many had their early training and experience in the personnel relations field; still others cut their teeth in consumer goods marketing, general management in almost any field, or management consulting. Almost all of the highly successful recruiters' backgrounds contain an exposure to sales of a product or service. Some are Ph.D. psychologists. At least one is a former medical doctor. A few are attorneys who either disliked or failed at law. Virtually all once were executives themselves. Not even a handful are trained engineers or accountants, whose tendencies to think more in the realm of black and white than of unpredictable human behavior tend to disqualify them from evaluating people expertly. Contrary to publicity, almost none are college students, temporarily unemployed, or housewives—the business is easy to crack, but not that easy.

Headhunters share other characteristics as well. They like to work on short-term assignments whose results can be quickly and observably measured and enjoyed. They have a penchant for living in suspense and by their wits, and they cannot abide for long in what they portray as the predictable stability that characterizes ordinary execu-tive jobs. They thrive on the stimulation and prestige of rubbing shoulders with industry, business and private sector decision makers and leaders; most can hold their liquor as well as or better than the candidates they interview. The successful ones are self-motivat-ed and compulsively hard working, accustomed to breakfast and dinner interviews, weekend phone calling and living out of a suitcase. They take vacations, but rare is the experienced headhunter who has not memorized area codes and most of his clients' phone numbers.

A few other attributes:

- Most have MBA's or equivalent levels of education
- Most are equipped to discuss detailed practices in a variety of businesses
- Most know the "buzzwords" of their client industries
- Most have excellent memories for names and faces
- They have mastered the art of the interview, armed with a battery of "who", "what", "when", "where", "why" and "how" questions designed to avoid the stereotypical yes or no answer
- They are adept at handholding cautious client company officers, having learned "the knack of explaining the inexplicable, placating the implacable, soothing the rough sea, or stirring up the mill pond to set client or candidate minds to rest."
- They are skilled negotiators; ready and able to discuss matters pertaining to salaries, fringe benefits, bonuses, stock options, and other imaginative forms of compensation to concoct pay packages that will attract the selected candidate.

Finally, Mr. Wilkinson observes: "headhunters pride themselves on being just plain good businessmen, and most are. On the whole, they are interesting people and real, and they count among their friends the business people with whom they have become close, clients and candidates alike."

CHAPTER 4
HOW EXECUTIVE RECRUITERS WORK

What you should know is that I'm probably no more
than two degrees of separation away from anybody I need
to contact–including Bill Gates.
– Mark Jaffe, Wyatt & Jaffe

hen working with any business, it helps to have insight into how that business works. That insight helps to work with that business effectively and have the right expectations for the result. If you're working with a bank, you should know what it does, what its services, features and policies are, and how to interact with it. And you may want to know what, exactly, it does with your money. If you don't, you may be in for a surprise the next time you need cash, a mortgage, or a credit line. You'll likely to be confused by its actions and communications. Results will differ from that expected. The same is true for executive recruiters–if you're working with one, or if one contacts you–and you don't understand how they operate, there is greater chance for failure.

This chapter explores the inner workings of the executive recruiting firm. The first part of the chapter examines the recruiter-client relationship and how it comes about. Next is a description of the executive recruiting process and how an executive placement might work, followed by a summary of the recruiter-candidate relationship and what you, as a potential candidate, can expect from it. Along the way, differences between retainer and contingency firms are pointed out. Important issues and considerations such as confidentiality, standards, ethics and governance are also highlighted. How recruiters are paid–which as you might expect, has a lot to do with how they operate–will also be covered. By the end of this chapter you should have a pretty good idea of what recruiters do and how they do it. With this knowledge you can move ahead to Part 3 to learn how to best work with them to achieve desired results.

THE CLIENT/RECRUITER RELATIONSHIP

Recall from Chapter 3 that the client in this case is the hiring company–that is, the company that needs to fill a position. The client firm engages the recruiter to help find candidates (job seekers) best suited for that position. Recall also that retained search firms are engaged exclusively to provide services often beyond the hiring itself–in fact, they are paid whether a candidate is hired or not. Retained firms generally operate in the higher level executive management "space" or with very specialized techni-cal positions. Contingency firms, on the other hand, do not get exclusive engagements, are paid only on placement, provide little service to the client beyond locating candidates, and operate generally at lower levels in the cor-porate hierarchy.

That short review allows us to move on to discuss how the client rela-tionship comes about and how it works. First, it is important to understand why a client company would need or use an executive recruiter in the first place. Then, it's important to understand how the deal gets done–how an executive recruiter is selected by the client and actually engaged. Having a firm grasp of the rationale and process for engaging a recruiter will offer clues as to how to work with the recruiter, what questions to ask, and what expectations to have.

Why Do Client Companies Use Recruiters?

Why do companies use executive recruiters? There are many reasons. They usually boil down to one or a combination of the following three things:

1. Confidentiality. There are many reasons why a company might want to fill a position without others in the company, or in the industry, being aware of the activity. Non-performance is an obvious case, where an executive or manager is deemed not to be performing as expected, and the replacement process if disclosed could become very touchy. A planned CEO secession or departure of a key executive, likewise, is often kept under wraps so as not to distress employees, shareholders, customers, investment bankers, and so forth. These issues are human-resource and personality driven, but there are also market-driven reasons as well. If a company is planning to start a new product line and wants to "hit the ground running" with a solid management team but doesn't want the news to leak, a confidential search is in order—particularly since the competition is a likely source of eligible candidates. Typically, these kinds of searches are done as blind searches—meaning the client company remains unidentified—and it is delicate ground for the recruiter, the client, and potential candidates. Mainly these searches involve the depth, careful planning and high degree of professional discretion found in retained search firms. The contingency search process—set up mainly for breadth and speed—doesn't lend itself well to confidentiality.

2. Economy—to save time and money. Particularly at higher levels in the organization, finding and hiring the right candidate can be a downright difficult and expensive process. Companies would have to maintain a staff of professional recruiters in an HR (human resources) capacity. For a variety of reasons, HR as a function in most corporations has evolved away from recruiting and into more administrative roles—administering benefit plans, government regulations, training and development. Most company HR departments simply don't have the bandwidth, time or network to deal with an extensive executive search. Managers and personnel in other functional parts of the organization have even less time or bandwidth, so the situation entails—as many others do in today's corporate America—an outsourcing of the activity to specialists. Further, it is harder for "internal" search processes to remain confidential. Finally, HR departments will usually take longer (time is money) and may not be able to locate as skilled a candidate, resulting in potentially costly mismatches.

3. Professional skills and knowledge. Executive recruiters are professionals. They are trained in and have experience in finding and screening candidates effectively for positions. They are focused 100 percent of the time on doing so. Perhaps most importantly, they have tools and networks for getting the job done—formal and informal contacts and resources located all over the country (and world) and in all industries to help them get the job done. Recruiters can also be effective, non-partial negotiators to deal with compensation, relocation, and other sensitive issues. Companies face the same "do-it-yourself" choice alluded to in Chapter 3—do it yourself and risk a poor fit or failure in a time-consuming job search, or turn it over to a professional. Increasingly—particularly in tight labor markets—engaging with professionals brings a more favorable outcome.

THE EXECUTIVE RECRUITING PROCESS

Recall that the "engagement" is between the recruiter and the client, or hiring company, not between the recruiter and the candidate. The engagement is part of a formal and deliberate strategy of the client firm to employ a recruiter to help fill, and possibly define, a position. Consequently, it makes sense to describe the steps of the recruiting process from the client point of view. The client will be part of, or at least informed of, every step in the process. As candidate, the process will only touch you in a few places. But it helps to know what goes on behind the scenes, so that you know where the recruiter and client company are "coming from" when they approach you. Of course, developing a relationship with the recruiter can help your chances, and a discussion of how this relationship works follows and is covered more in Part 3.

As you learn the recruiting process, keep in mind that the process naturally varies a lot by situation, history, client company, type of recruiter and specific recruiting firm and personnel involved. A retained search typically follows a series of steps similar to the following (similarities and differences between retained and contingency search will be highlighted and discussed along the way):

- Recruiter selection and engagement
- Review and understand position context
- Define the position
- Identify potential candidates
- Review candidates and decide whom to contact

- Approach candidates
- Bring client and candidates together
- Make selection (s)
- Check references ("vet" the candidate)
- Make offer and negotiate
- Follow up

This section gives a framework for each step in the recruiting process. Again, it can vary a lot by the situation and history between the client and recruiter. The focus here is not to train you to be a recruiter–rather to help you to understand the process well enough to work effectively with it.

Select and Engage With Recruiter

Obviously, at this stage the client company has decided it has a position to fill from outside the company. This decision can emerge from a variety of situations, the detail of which is beyond the scope of this book. Most commonly, positions arise either from departure, expected or planned departure, expected or planned secession (especially at higher executive levels), or expansion in the business. There can be special situations arising from new business situations, new technologies, mergers and acquisitions, or compliance with new laws or regulations that cause a company to "go to market" to seek new talent. Often, when an executive recruiter is employed, there is a need to find a candidate that will "hit the ground running"–a candidate who already possesses skills and experience in the type of position being recruited. Recruiters are less likely to be employed to bring "green" staff or trainees into an organization.

Client firms select recruiters based on a number of factors. First and foremost is the relationship a firm may already have with the recruiter. A long-standing relationship means that the recruiter already understands the corporate climate and needs of the organization. A familiar recruiter is in a better position to find a good fit quickly and efficiently. Not surprisingly, executive recruiting firms strive for long-term relationships with their clients. Repeat business is highly desirable. Good recruiting firms will do what is necessary to please the client firm–so while it is true that retained recruiters are paid regardless of hire, they know that good long-term relationships are built upon successful placements.

Recruiting firms–and especially retained search firms–are engaged much as any other consultant might be engaged. Long-term relationships are a big factor. Experience in the industry, skills, knowledge, networks, characteristics of individual recruiters and specialization with particular types of jobs will all enter into recruiter selection. More than one recruiter may be asked to develop proposals for how to handle a specific recruiting assignment. Each recruiter will make their "pitch" in what is sometimes termed as a "shootout" and a selection will be made. With retained search, once a recruiter is selected, that selection is exclusive for a period of time, usually three to four months but possibly longer depending on the assignment.

Contingency recruiter engagement may also be based on long-term relationships and success with a client. But more often, the strategy behind a contingency search is to (1) achieve breadth–to cast a wide net to locate candidates, (2) to hone in on specific professions and skill sets through the use of specialists, and (3) to get it done quickly. So the client firm will look for the recruiter(s) who can best do the job at that time for that position. The relationship is not exclusive–often more than one contingency firm is engaged for a position. Contingency recruiter engagement is more of an "outsourcing" arrangement, while retained recruiters are engaged more as "consultants."

Cost may also be a factor. The client firm, by choosing a contingency recruiter, is willing to pay only if someone is hired and is generally not interested in paying for any services beyond searching for candidates. Although recruiter fees are fairly standardized, there is no formal or industry standard fee schedule, and there is some price competition. A typical fee is 30-33 percent of the hired executive's total first-year compensation.

Review and Understand Position Context

Before setting out to find candidates, the recruiter (a good one, anyway) will spend intensive time and energy with the client to understand the position, how it came open, and the organizational context and culture in which the position operates. Appropriately called by some the "due diligence immersion," the recruiter interviews key stakeholders all over the organization to get a better sense of what is sought, what will work, and what will not work. The recruiter talks to people directly connected with the position function, as well as such "indirect" stakeholders as the HR manager. The recruiter assesses what skills–both tangible and intangible–are important for success in the position. The recruiter also gets a firm grasp on how much confidentiality is required. If the search is sensitive and must be kept under wraps, the recruiter must know from the beginning. Situation assessment is particularly tricky with higher-level positions, where intangible attributes such as personality, leadership and charisma are so important. It is not hard to see how a recruiter with a long history with a client has an advantage. Retained recruiters will spend much more time and energy on this stage, with personal visits to the client site considered to be indispensable.

Define the Position

As an executive recruiting function, this step is almost exclusively the bailiwick of the retained search firm. With contingency searches, this part is almost always complete. Retained search firms are usually working in the higher ranges of the corporate ladder, where positions must be very carefully defined and customized for every situation. Where necessary, the recruiter will work together with the client company to define specific job responsibilities, skill and personality requirements necessary for success. Recruiters can add a lot of value, for clients fail to spend enough time in this area or are too close to the situation to do it effectively. Some companies assume the new candidate must possess exactly the same skills and fit the same job as the former position holder, where a more realistic outside assessment may reveal valuable differences that should be taken into account. Experienced executive recruiters are good at this exercise, for they have not only the experience, objectivity, and insight to work through this stage, but also the motivation–the more the client and recruiter are on the same page, the greater the chance for success. Further, many executive recruiters were formerly management consultants and have dealt deeply with position definition and fit in other corporations. Smart client companies will bring them into the position definition process, and smart consultants will gladly help out.

Identify Potential Candidates

Here is where the rubber meets the road and where the recruiter "value add" really starts to show. Once the recruiter has a pretty good idea of the position, what the position requires, and the situation and context, they will kick their search apparatus into gear to identify all potential candidates. The process of identifying candidates combines art and science, networks and acquaintances with pure factual information.

Most recruiters maintain a database of potential candidates, gathered from submitted resumes, referrals, organization charts, professional organization membership lists, local business journals' "who's who in business" columns, and a variety of other sources. This database is usually the first stop for any recruiter. The recruiting professional will search by job title, skills, geography, or any other attribute relevant to the search.

But the search seldom ends with a database search. If that were the case, the recruiter's job would be too easy—and the client firm could satisfy their needs simply by buying the data. Effective searches typically go well beyond the candidate database. Once the database resource is exhausted, the recruiter will turn into private investigator, wringing and decoding information from all possible sources. The recruiter may already know the industry in depth if he specializes in it, or he will study the industry and detailed Form 10-K annual reports from firms in similar industries, especially for senior executives whose names will often be in the report. But the search usually goes well beyond these tools as well. Most searches entail at least some contact with individuals. The "network" is an all-important source.

Searching the network is a learned art in the recruiting world. Experienced recruiters spend a lot of time building the network—acquiring key contacts in key places within the industries they specialize. They may call a candidate for a job one day, then use that individual as a source of referrals the next. Good recruiters have key contacts in the right places, and they do what they can to maintain and nourish that network. Finding jobs, finding jobs for friends, a gift or a lunch here and there—all part of keeping the network alive and productive. Through the network, they know who is who and where, what their intentions are, and so forth. They try to know who is advancing, who has been passed over, and who may be looking for a job within the "source" organizations they work with. Typically, the recruiter will use these tools to identify a short list of candidates (a few, to a few dozen) to consider contacting directly.

Recruiters—especially larger firms—keep specialized staff on their payroll. They may have employees that do nothing but research—culling the database, looking at industry publications and the like to fill specific positions—or keep the database up to date. There may be another level of "junior" employees who do nothing but place initial calls to candidates—or to people who might know the candidates. The professional recruiter may sit in the background and wait for all of this to occur and for the candidate list to be created and narrowed before talking with candidates directly.

Reviewing Candidates

All of this work—and still a bit more—happens in the background well before a candidate is even contacted. Particularly in a retained search, there is no point calling candidates and bringing them to the table if not a good fit. So the recruiter wants to play their cards wisely and not waste effort calling candidates who don't fit or who aren't interested. Likewise, the client firm wants tightly screened candidates—not a steady parade of interviewees. So once the recruiting firm draws up a screened list of top candidates, they bring it to the client firm, and together they go through the resumes and profiles of each candidate, narrowing the list down still further. At the end of that exercise, the list is usually down to a few candidates. Note that this process is more likely to occur in a retained search—in a contingency search there may be less collaborative work to screen down the list of contacted candidates—or there may be none at all. The client firm pays only upon hire—but may expend time and energy interviewing more marginal candidates.

Approaching Candidates

Now the recruiting firm has a short list, and they begin to contact candidates. The tactics again can vary by the type and level and position and the industry, and the need for confidentiality. Typically the recruiter or an associate or "developer" in the office calls the candidate at work and notifies him or her of a potential opportunity. They either talk about it there or set up time off-line—after work, at breakfast, lunch or dinner—to discuss it further, if the candidate is interested. If the potential candidate is not interested, the recruiter will usually try to bring him into the network and ask if he/she knows anyone who might be. If the candidate is a "new" contact, the recruiter, all through this process, tries to establish rapport with the potential candidate for future positions and referrals.

As a candidate, if you sent a resume into the search firm and are already part of their database, you may have had a preliminary or "courtesy" interview already. If that's not the case, the recruiter will usually try to set up an exploratory interview over the phone (if you are a very high-level executive, this interview may be in person, with the recruiter traveling to your location). This interview might be 20 minutes to half an hour or longer. The recruiter will attempt to verify both your credentials and your interest. If one or both are lacking, the recruiter may still ask for referrals (whether you give any should be carefully thought out based on the reputation and intentions of the recruiter–it may make sense to learn who the recruiter is and call back later).

If a match does appear to be in the making, the recruiter may then do a full-blown telephone interview. By now, as a candidate you've probably been screened down from a list of perhaps several hundred from a database to a short list of perhaps 10 or fewer candidates. If high-level executives are involved, there will likely be an in-person in-depth interview with the

Figure 4-1. Typical Executive Recruiting "Funnel"

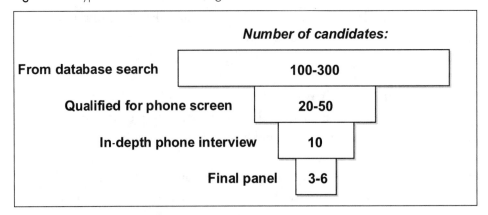

recruiter to develop a final group or panel of perhaps up to six candidates to present to the client firm.

Bringing the Client and Candidates Together

At this point, the recruiter has done most of his/her work—a panel of perhaps three to six highly qualified candidates has been brought back to the client company. Some clients may want to get involved more deeply in selecting the semifinalists. These clients will get more involved in the interviewing and screening process described above. Panel candidates are brought back to the client company for in-person interviews with individual executives. In some cases, an internal search committee does the interviews. The recruiter plays a "back seat" role, helping with logistics and providing a "dossier" of background information to the client.

Making the Selection(s)

The client firm, with interviews and background information available, selects the perceived best candidate (and often a runner-up). Again, the recruiter stays mainly in the background but may give advice or facilitate the decision process.

Checking References

Reference checks may occur at different stages of the process. The reference check, sometimes known as "vetting" the candidate, will be very thorough for a chosen candidate, even to the point of checking the references. Particularly when confidential searches are involved, reference checks must be handled delicately. Using references from the client firm can give away intentions and can derail the effort if done unscrupulously at the candidate's former firm (a good counter-offer can change the candidate's mind, for example). Some recruiters look for social or non-professional references, or otherwise completely disguise their intentions.

Making an Offer

With or without the recruiter's help, the client firm will make an offer. Many retained search firms are involved in establishing the offer and the

negotiation of terms with the candidate, although both offer and acceptance are the final prerogative of the client and candidate.

Follow Up

Good recruiters will follow the progress of the hired candidate with the
client organization. Not only is this a goodwill gesture to help entrench the
recruiter with the client, but it also helps the recruiter to be more effective
with the next search. Good recruiters will also give feedback to candidates
not chosen – particularly final panelists–so as to keep the door open for the
next opportunity. The recruiter who burns bridges–either with clients or
candidates–doesn't survive long in the business.

THE CANDIDATE/RECRUITER RELATIONSHIP

The relationship formed between you as candidate and the recruiter will
vary widely depending on your own credentials and interests, the recruiter
and their processes, and the job market. As mentioned in Chapter 3, you
are not the customer, rather you are part of the product. Many recruiters
will only work with you when you are the right "product" to fill a specific
customer need. Other recruiters will want to "stock" you on the shelf in
case the right customer walks in the door. Those recruiters will keep an
"inventory" of good candidates in their database and may work with you
in advance of specific customers or positions in mind. Generally, contingency search firms fall into this category. For them, keeping an inventory
means faster placements and less time and effort spent on the phone
searching for candidates.

Generally you will not sign an agreement or "exclusive" with a recruiting firm. If you work with a contingency firm, you are free to work with
more than one firm, and your resume and profile could be shared with
hundreds of firms, often without your knowledge. While increasing
breadth, keeping confidentiality is difficult–your resume may even end up
back at your own firm! Retained search firms, on the other hand, will work
less with "inventory" and more with direct contact and will contact you
generally about a specific position with one firm only.

There is a lot of debate on the issue of just how active–and proac-
tive–to be with executive recruiters. In some cases you'll be rewarded for

your efforts; in others you may become just a number and a nuisance for the recruiter. In Chapters 5-8 we'll explore the mechanics and do's and don'ts of getting visibility and results through an executive recruiter.

STANDARDS, ETHICS AND GOVERNANCE

The executive recruiting industry often has been criticized for unscrupulous actions and behaviors, ranging from invasion of privacy to providing misleading information to clients and candidates and "selling" unqualified candidates into positions. The lure of lucrative contracts and "easy money" from quick matches has indeed been too strong for some to ignore, and as in most anything else, the bad behaviors of a few can taint the entire industry.

Unlike many other professions, such as public accounting or law, there are indeed no established standards for compliance in the executive recruiting profession. There is no licensing, examination, or state board for recruiting firms and their recruiters. Reputation thus becomes the primary self-policing process. A bad reputation will quickly spread among client firms, and business will suffer for those recruiters. Unfortunately, it is more difficult for candidates to keep track of recruiter reputations.

Fortunately, recognizing the unregulated state of affairs, two different professional associations have formed to develop processes, codes of ethics and otherwise assist the recruiting industry: the Association of Executive Search Consultants and the International Association of Corporate and

Code of Ethics: Every profession has found it necessary to establish a code of ethics as a necessary part of the process of self-discipline and to protect the interests of clients and assure them of fair treatment. A code of professional ethics helps the practitioner determine the propriety of his conduct in his professional relationships. It indicates the kind of professional posture the practitioner must develop and maintain if he is to succeed. It gives the clients and potential clients a basis for feeling confident that the professional person desires to serve them well and places services ahead of financial reward. It gives clients assurance that the professional person will do his work in conformity with professional standards of competence, independence and integrity. The Association of Executive Search Consultants Code of Ethics is followed by many executive recruiting consultants in North America.

Professional Recruitment. When selecting a recruiting firm, it makes sense to note whether the firm is a member of AESC or the recruiters are members of IACPR.

Association of Executive Search Consultants (AESC)

The AESC has crafted and distributed a detailed code of ethics and professional practice guidelines to the industry. The detail is located in the Appendix. The topics addressed include:

- Professionalism
- Integrity
- Competence
- Objectivity
- Accuracy

- Conflicts of Interest
- Confidentiality
- Loyalty
- Equal Opportunity
- Public Interest

As you work with recruiters you might want to ask if they follow the guidelines. If you work with recruiters frequently, you may want to get more familiar with these or similar guidelines and the AESC itself. A Web

Figure 4-2. AESC front page.

site with more detail available on the recruiting industry and practice is available at www.aesc.org.

International Association of Corporate and Professional Recruitment (IACPR)

IACPR is another industry association serving the recruiting community and client human resources managers who work with recruiters. Its role and objective go beyond standards and governance: "to share information pertinent to the recruitment, selection, retention and development of senior executives." The Web site is www.iacpr.org.

Figure 4-3. IACPR front page.

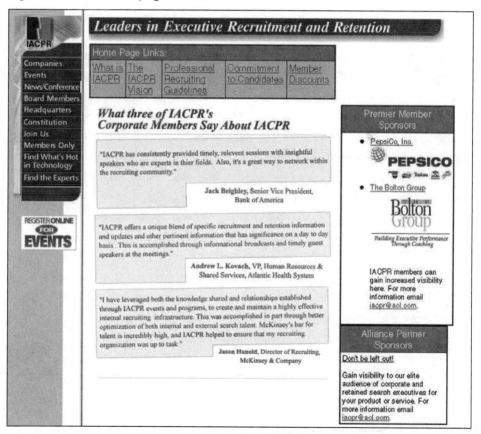

To work effectively with executive recruiters, it is important to know how they operate and to understand the relationship between them and their client companies. The exact steps will vary by position, situation, and whether it is a retained or contingency search. Although the industry has no established licensing or legal standards, industry trade associations AESC and IACPR help to standardize and facilitate the recruiting process.

How, and How Much, Do Executive Recruiters Get Paid?

Executive recruiter compensation can vary somewhat but is usually based on a percentage of the expected first year salary for the position involved. The typical fee is one-third of the expected first year salary for a single position. Thus, for a position paying $150,000 annually, the recruiter can expect a fee of $50,000. Note that the retained search firm receives the fee whether or not a candidate is hired, while the contingency firm only gets paid upon hire—no hire, no fee, period. Note also that some retained search firms effectively set their salary level floor by imposing a minimum fee. A minimum of $50K or $60K would induce clients to use them only for assignments with salaries of $150K or $180K and up. Many contingency search agreements call for a probationary period after the hire, where all or part of a fee can be refunded if the placement doesn't work out (a necessary "quality control" device). Among contingency firms there may be price competition, driving the fee down as low as 20% of first year salary—although quality and due diligence may come into question. Both retained and contingency firms may give price breaks for multiple searches or multiple positions. Retained search firms may also bill for out-of-pocket expenses, such as travel for recruiting personnel and candidates. Typically if a hire is not made during the retainer period, a retained recruiter will continue the search with only out-of-pocket expenses incurred. If the search is terminated early (for instance, if an internal candidate is hired), the fee will be prorated to the period of time in which the search is active. Some retained search firms may bill by task or time units for consulting work, such as position planning or compensation strategy, although often it is included in the base agreement. As a candidate, understanding how the recruiter is paid gives insight into client firm and recruiter motives and actions.

PART 3
WORKING WITH
RECRUITING
FIRMS

CHAPTER 5
SELECTING AND CONTACTING
EXECUTIVE RECRUITERS

Avoid the mistake of asking: "What did you think of my resume?" Get advice from your first boss or wife (may be the same person), or from Aunt Alice the English teacher, but don't expect the recruiter to be your personal career counselor.
– James H. Kennedy, founding editor of
Executive Recruiter News.

t's an age-old discussion. When considering a job change, do you contact an executive recruiter, or is it better to wait for them to contact you? Does it matter who you are and what kind of position you are looking for? Whether or not you're currently employed? And if you decide it is best to contact a recruiter, how do you select the recruiter or recruiters to contact? How many recruiters, and why? And once the choice is made, how do you initiate the contact and the relationship?

These questions are difficult, and there are a lot of subtle issues to consider in answering them. A slight miss can make all the difference in the world in starting and completing an effective job search. This chapter will address these concerns and help you build a recruiter contact strategy–when to contact recruiters, which recruiters to contact and how. You'll learn about tools to help select and contact recruiters. Finally, you'll learn how to open a recruiter relationship and learn what to expect in the beginning.

WHEN–AND WHEN NOT–TO INITIATE A RECRUITER RELATIONSHIP

As a natural step in your position search, you would probably expect to contact executive recruiters. You would expect to contact those most likely to have the positions available that match your needs and interests. You would expect to use Kennedy Information's *Directory of Executive Recruiters* and related resources to identify those recruiters, then to methodically contact them to let them know you're available and advise them of your credentials.

The reality is that this last statement may or may not be true, or may be true in part. As a candidate, you should prepare to contact executive recruiters, and you should know "who's who" and who may be best suited to find the appropriate position. But you should know upfront that large recruiting firms receive thousands of resumes every week, and even small boutique firms may receive hundreds each week. It is wrong to assume that all recruiters want to hear from you. Depending on a wide variety of factors, they may or may not want you to contact them. With retained search for senior executives, the process is usually more a "search" than a "placement," and sending unsolicited material may at best do no good and at worst be annoying and counterproductive. With mid-level positions and most contingency search, recruiters will accept your resume, but the process will be much more effective if you use the right contact strategy. How do you know when to contact executive recruiters, and what is the best way to do it?

How Do Recruiters Want to Deal With You?

Recall from Chapters 3 and 4 the unique business model of the recruiting industry–where the client firm is the customer and you are the product. As product, the recruiter has a choice of "inventory" models with respect to how they manage you. They can "stock" you, that is, put you in inventory and wait for an order or a client position to open up. Or they can first receive the order, then go about acquiring you, the product, to fulfill that order. Whether or not to contact a recruiting firm depends a lot on which model it uses.

The general rule is: the higher the level you are at, and the higher the level the recruiting firm deals with, the more likely the "build to order" model is in effect. At the highest levels (salary $150K and above), most recruiters shy away from keeping resumes on file for three reasons. First, "stock" inventory seldom fits the need for very high level, specialized positions, thus a candidate search would probably occur anyway. Second, a candidate sending a resume might appear a little more needy, particularly an unemployed candidate, who may actually be looked at as "damaged goods." Clients expect recruiters to earn their fees by locating and recruiting top candidates, not to collect $25K or $50K to check the unemployment line. Third, it is difficult to keep resumes on file up to date. The recruiter can't trust the resume to be current, and it probably isn't. As a result, high-end executive search firms typically discourage unsolicited resumes, and if they do keep them, may only keep them on file for a short time, usually six months or less.

On the other hand, contingency search firms and retained search firms working lower-level, $100K-or-less positions will keep an active database and put most resumes on file. These databases have sophisticated classification systems, and recruiters use them regularly to search for a match and start building lists of candidates to contact. The fastest way for them to fill an order is to take stock off the shelf, with some value added in the form of screening, interviewing, and validating credentials to match the candidate with the position.

Some firms may operate with a blend of both business models; that is, use "stock" resumes along with an active search to get the best slate of candidates. As databases become more sophisticated and more up-to-date (driven in part by the availability of candidate information from the Internet) and as clients demand faster placements, stock resumes become more important in the search process.

Completion Rate.

Percentage of retained searches that result in a hire. Estimated to be as low as 60 percent, claimed to be as high as 100 percent (be wary of the latter: no one is perfect, and the imponderables/ intangibles in a search are many). Greatly affected by client lassitude in interviewing and following up with candidates, changes (written and subtle) in job specifications, internal client politics, organizational changes, etc....as well as by recruiter performance and effectiveness.

Deciding to Contact a Recruiter–
Factors to Consider

How do you know whether to contact a particular recruiter with your unsolicited resume? Some firms may offer a direct answer. Check the Web site–many recruiters post what they look for and explain how to submit resumes. You can also call. Usually a receptionist or administrative person will answer, and you can ask if resumes are accepted. They might ask some questions about credentials and the position you seek. It's probably not a good idea to call individual recruiting professionals themselves–they don't have the time, they don't know who you are and, remember, their first interest is filling open positions for clients, not finding a job for you.

Beyond these two approaches, it is a guessing game–but you can increase the odds by making an educated guess. Which recruiters will keep you "in stock" even if there are no current positions available? In many situations the recruiter benefits from holding you as inventory, even if that transcends their normal process. The following factors make recruiters more likely to keep you "on the shelf":

■ **Credentials.** Your credentials are pristine and highly sought after. No recruiter would discard Jack Welch's resume.

■ **Position level and salary.** You have "CEO," "COO," or "VP" in your title, make more than $150K a year, and work for a successful "marquis" name like Dell, Starbucks or Wal-Mart. Your resume is less likely to be discarded, but, that said, most high-level recruiters know who you are without the use of an unsolicited resume. Still, most retained and contingency firms would want to keep your resume on file. If your background and resume speak to excellence, most recruiters will want to see it, and many will keep it.

■ **Job market.** If the economy and employment market is booming, "orders" are many and "inventory" is scarce. Thus, recruiters are more likely to "stock up" when the opportunity presents itself. Likewise, in a downturn–just when more candidates are available and sending resumes, recruiters are less likely to need them and keep them. More farsighted, long-term-oriented recruiters may keep them on file awaiting the upturn–particularly if the other factors are in your favor.

- **Job status.** You're unemployed. "Unemployed" is a yellow flag for a recruiter, meaning possible "damaged goods" to a recruiter. Recruiters don't want damaged goods in stock. If you're unemployed–first of all, don't be–do something useful even if for free. Secondly, make it clear that the reason for unemployment is systemic, that is, due to the economic situation of your company, and not because of you. If it is because of you, your situation is difficult, but don't try to disguise it because most recruiters will figure it out. Explain your situation, and expect that many recruiters will decline to keep you on file. Many retained search firms will dismiss you right away, because clients would dismiss you right off a final search panel.

- **Field.** If you're an accomplished research fellow in nuclear medicine, you just might want to send that resume. Firms–particularly those that specialize in a field–like to carry inventory on scarce product available in that field.

Sometimes your best "fit" into a recruiter's scheme–for now–is as a source of referrals. Recruiters may hang on to your credentials just for that purpose. At this stage, that's OK. It builds your credibility and relationship with a recruiter–and sooner or later it will be your turn. Chapter 7 discusses this idea further–it may be whom you know as much as what you know. It's a good idea to identify, at least in your cover letter, where and for whom you work in your current organization. If your first few contacts with a recruiter seem to be only to gather references, don't despair. You're building a relationship–and you're in the system.

FORMING A RECRUITER CONTACT STRATEGY

If you decide that it makes sense to contact recruiters, the next questions are how many, which ones, and how. Modern computer and Internet-aided tools accommodate 5,000-resume mass mailings, but is this the right path? The general rule: it is best to focus, or target your search somewhat, but the dimensions of your search depend on many factors. A more selective and personal approach is often more advisable than a press release. Some determining factors relate to you, your situation and objectives. Some relate to the recruiter landscape—how recruiters are structured and how they do business. In general, a recruiter contact strategy consists of three parts:

1. **Identify**. Identify which recruiters offer the highest potential to work with you, based on your field, background, needs, and geographic location.
2. **Contact**. Contact selected recruiters by sending a resume and cover letter.
3. **Follow up.** Keep in touch with most promising recruiters, nurture the working relationship.

Identifying Recruiters: How Many?

The decision to do a mass versus a targeted mailing depends in part on your situation and what you're trying to accomplish. If you're a mid-level candidate completely certain that you need a new position ASAP and aren't worried about making it known, a broader, mass search will get you there faster. If you're content with where you are but want to be available for better opportunities, a narrower, more specialized search is in order. Likewise, if your skills and credentials, level, or geographic preferences are specialized, your search will be narrower. Generally, the following factors influence the breadth of a search:

■ **Confidentiality**. The more you circulate your resume, the more known it becomes that you're looking. Networks work, and the "buzz" spreads. Some recruiters are more careful than others about to which clients they send resumes. It happens—a candidate's name shows up on a list at his own firm! Working with one firm, closely and carefully, is the best way to keep tracks covered.

■ **Urgency**. If you need something to happen fast—either because of your personal situation or a situation at your employer—a broader search typically gets faster results. If you anticipate a downturn in your company or your industry and want to hit the exit before others, it doesn't hurt to cast a broad net. Recruiters also know about these downturns—and if you're early, it shows that you are aware of the situation and more likely a better candidate. Likewise, if you're moving to a new area—perhaps as a trailing spouse—it makes sense to cast a broad net to recruiters working in that area.

- **Active vs. passive.** Activity relates both to urgency and confidentiality. If you wish to be active in your search, pressing all possibilities, a wider search is in order. If you want to take a passive approach simply to be made aware of new opportunities when they come up, it makes sense to pick out one recruiter or maybe a handful. A wide search may bring more interviews and discussions than you can handle while still functioning in a current position.

- **Your value in the market.** Don't commoditize yourself. Launching a broad campaign can make you appear as a commodity. The law of diminishing returns sets in–sending resumes to twice as many recruiters probably results in only 5 percent more interviews. Many recruiters recommend a more personal approach. You tend to appear as more valuable if positioning yourself as the one sought rather than the seeker, one who values the contact and relationship with a recruiter or limited set of recruiters, one who wants only that special, coveted position. Be advised though, particularly with contingency firms, that a broad cast creates competition and a sense of urgency among recruiters. If your credentials are good, they want to place you before someone else does. If you're a mid-level candidate looking for quick results you may discard the selective approach in favor of taking advantage of the competitive situation.

Identifying Recruiters: Which Ones?

As you develop your contact strategy, the last step before going to selection tools is to think through just what kind of recruiter is best suited for your position search. Here, mainly as review, are some final things to think about:

- **Retained vs. contingency.** Retained search firms primarily deal with executive level managers or technical specialists, with salaries of $100K and up. If you're below this range, you're more likely to work with a contingency firm. If you are new in your career or in a high-turnover industry, such as health care or retail, you are also more likely to work with contingency recruiters. As a general rule, you will get more attention and assistance from contingency recruiters. The line between retained and contingency firms is becoming more blurred, as more firms are doing both. If you want "deep" consideration, exclusivity and confidentiality, you should contact retained recruiters. But don't contact a retainer firm used by your employer–they will not work with you. If you want broad reach, fast placement, and are willing to explore jobs that may not be a perfect fit, contingency firms will work. And remember–contingency firms are more likely to hang on to your material and keep you "in stock" if there is no current position available.

- **Specialty vs. general, and boutique versus large firms.** If you're looking for a firm with strong contacts in the industry or profession of your choice, a speciality firm is an obvious choice. But the flip side is that while specialists have excellent contacts in the industry, they are less likely to open new doors for you in other industries. Also keep in mind that many generalist firms really operate like a department store of specialist or boutique firms. That is, by working with a generalist you may get the advantages of specialization along with the broader set of possibilities offered by a generalist. Boutique firms will tend to get you better matches and work more closely with you to achieve your goals, but your credentials must be right to get their attention. Many recruiters recommend working with a mix of specialists and generalists.

- **Functional specialists vs. industry specialists.** Is it better to work with a functional specialist–that is, a recruiter working with your profession (accounting, finance, marketing, IT) or an industry specialist (aerospace, computers, food, financial services, etc.). The conventional wisdom: both dimensions are relevant, and it makes sense to work all recruiters where your credentials fit.

- **Individual recruiters vs. recruiting firms.** As you look through recruiter selection resources such as the Kennedy Information's *Directory of Executive Recruiters*, you'll see recruiting firms and the names of individual recruiters within those firms. In the "Specialties" index, you'll see individual names, then the firms. In most other places in the guide, the indexing points to the firm, not the individual. If you have the credentials and are looking for placement in the specialty, such as publishing or logistics, it may make sense to go to the individual. Keep in mind–while these special recruiters may look out for you and develop a more personal relationship, you may never get into a database. If that individual has no opening at the time, they may not bother to put you "into the system" for others in the firm. But to get a first chance at an available opportunity, you're in better shape to go to the individual recruiter directly. If you're trying to put yourself "on the shelf" for upcoming opportunities, you may be better off to send your material to the firm. Also, keep in mind that the firm is always there—but individuals change.

■ **Geography.** Obviously, if you have specific geographic preferences or objectives, it makes sense to deal with recruiters in that area. Or if desired positions reside in a locale, it makes sense to work with recruiters in that locale. Technology executives or professionals would gravitate towards recruiters in Silicon Valley or other high-tech locales; aerospace professionals towards Seattle, Southern California, or certain Midwestern cities. Again, often a composite broad-and-narrow approach works best. Some recruiters suggest contacting one recruiter in each region—that way you get broader coverage while maintaining a more exclusive approach to working in each region. But keep in mind that most recruiters, though located in a region, work nationally. They will have positions available from other regions.

■ **Branch vs. central office.** For large recruiting firms with branch offices, do you send resumes to each branch office or to a central headquarters location? Recruiters recommend sending to branch offices to get faster visibility with recruiters working actual positions. Those recruiters may not search central databases if they feel the right candidates are available locally. But the downside: branch office recruiters may not bother to put you in the central database. Again, a blended strategy may be best.

■ **Professionalism of recruiter.** Obviously you want to select recruiters with a high degree of respect and professionalism in the business. They will attract the best clients and positions and deal fewer surprises. Although there is no way to ascertain professionalism, particularly of individuals, membership in AESC or IACPR is an indicator. Word of mouth, previous placements, and time in the business all are factors. Once contact is established, many candidates interview their recruiters to confirm this important criterion.

IDENTIFYING SPECIFIC RECRUITERS

By now you have a pretty good idea what to look for as you begin to approach recruiters. Now the question becomes: which actual recruiters should you contact? How do you select those recruiters and get the appropriate contact information to direct your resume and cover letter?

There are numerous ways to find recruiting firms, both in print and online. The first recruiters to select and contact are those with matching positions available. Recruiting firms may advertise for a match position—in the *Wall Street Journal*, in a trade publication related to your industry, or on their Web site. With due care about confidentiality, these are obvious places to send your resume. The upside: these are recruiters who have positions, and you always want to work with recruiters who have positions. But the downside: ads bring a lot of candidate competition out of the bushes.

Beyond solicited positions, you must now select from the hundreds of recruiting firms using your criteria. Kennedy Information provides three excellent tools that lie at the heart of the recruiter selection process; indeed this book is designed to accompany these resources and prepare you to use them.

Figure 5-1. Kennedy's *Directory of Executive Recruiters*

Kennedy Information's *Directory of Executive Recruiters*

Chances are, when you acquired this book you were already aware of Kennedy's *Directory of Executive Recruiters* (known in the trade as the "Red Book"). The 1,200-page guide, updated annually, is a comprehensive source of recruiter information organized to help you identify recruiters using a number of criteria.

The first half of the book identifies and profiles over 5,700 recruiting firms, and is organized into retained

Figure 5.2: kennedyinfo.com Main Page

and contingency sections. For each recruiting firm, the profile includes full contact information and a short description of its business and areas of focus. Other factors as appropriate and supplied by the firms are listed: key contacts, functions (professional fields such as marketing, finance, IT), industries (businesses such as automotive, aerospace and financial services, or "generalist"), salary ranges, geographic focus, branch offices, and professional affiliations (such as AESC). (For a more complete breakdown of functions and industries, see Appendix TK.)

You can thumb through the manual or use the special indexes to select recruiters. Special indexes are available by function, industry, recruiter specialty (the listings are by individual recruiter instead of firm) and geography. You'll find the Directory to be easy to use, informative and self-explanatory. But for a more automated approach, Kennedy also provides web and software-based tools based on the same database that produces the

Directory. These tools automate recruiter selection based on criteria you supply and can be used to automate the contact process as well.

Kennedy's Executive Recruiter Database

Kennedy Information operates a complete information resource on the Web at www.KennedyInfo.com. This site is partitioned into numerous resources for both candidates and recruiters.

As a candidate, the most useful resources are located in the section called "Executive Career Management." Located within this section are three information tools: Executive Recruiter Database, ExecutiveAgent.com, and

Figure 5.3: Kennedy Executive Recruiter Database Search

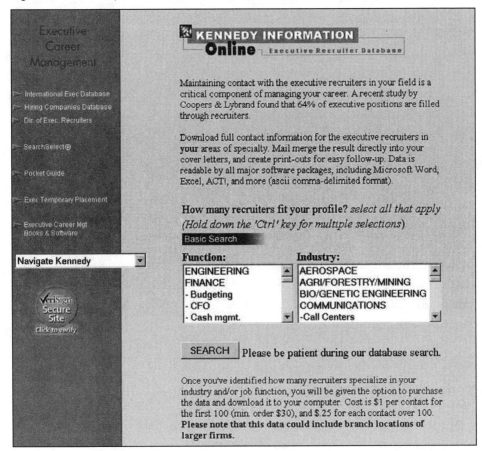

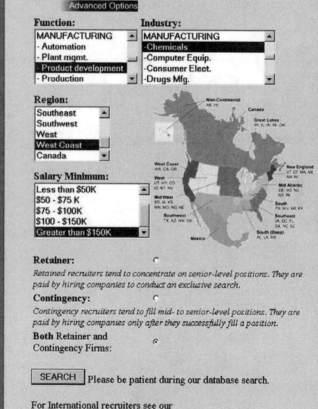

Executive
Career
Management

▸ Exec. Recruiter Database

▸ Hiring Companies Database

▸ Dir. of Exec. Recruiters

▸ SearchSelect®

▸ Pocket Guide

▸ Exec Temporary Placement

▸ Executive Career Mgt
  Books & Software

VeriSign
Secure
Site
Click to verify

KENNEDY INFORMATION
Online Executive Recruiter Database

Advanced Search

Use this screen to refine your search further.

Remember: recruiters work for hiring companies -- not you as a job-seeker -- so it is in your best interest to distribute your resume to as many appropriate recruiters as possible.

Once you've identified the right recruiters, purchase the data and download it right to your computer. Cost is $1 per name for the first 100 (min. order $30), and $.25 for each contact over 100. **Please note that this data could include branch locations of larger firms.**

How many recruiters fit your profile? *select all that apply*
(Hold down the 'Ctrl' key for multiple selections)

Advanced Options

Function:
MANUFACTURING
- Automation
- Plant mgmt.
- Product development
- Production

Industry:
MANUFACTURING
-Chemicals
-Computer Equip.
-Consumer Elect.
-Drugs Mfg.

Region:
Southeast
Southwest
West
West Coast
Canada

Salary Minimum:
Less than $50K
$50 - $75 K
$75 - $100K
$100 - $150K
Greater than $150K

Retainer:
Retained recruiters tend to concentrate on senior-level positions. They are paid by hiring companies to conduct an exclusive search.

Contingency:
Contingency recruiters tend to fill mid- to senior-level positions. They are paid by hiring companies only after they successfully fill a position.

Both Retainer and
Contingency Firms:

SEARCH | Please be patient during our database search.

For International recruiters see our
International Database of Executive Recruiters

Figure 5.4. Kennedy Executive Recruiter Database Search–Advanced

SearchSelect 3.0, along with an assortment of other available print resources. Each tool is designed to automate recruiter identification and contact. These resources are particularly helpful to narrow down a handful of recruiters quickly and to manage a large or protracted search campaign.

The Executive Recruiter Database

The executive recruiter database is the source for the Directory. Additionally, on the Web site, Kennedy makes an online search and select tool available, streamlining the thumb-through process. Enter your search criteria, and Kennedy returns the number of recruiters that meet your criteria. If you want specific names, there is a modest fee of $1 per name up to 100

Figure 5.5. Executive Recruiter Database result

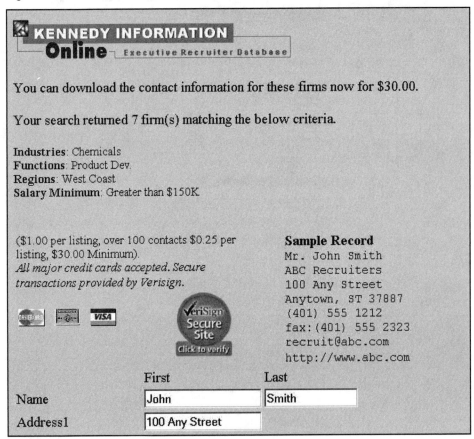

and $0.25 per name above 100. Thus, most selects done this way may cost a few dollars to a hundred or more. Obviously, the more specific the selection criteria, the more cost effective.

The basic database search allows you to search by function and industry. However, the more precise "Advanced Search" allows additional selection by type of recruiter (retained or contingency), geography and/or salary minimum. The advance search is highly recommended as it is both more precise and more economical. Following is an example of an advanced search done to find recruiters, both retained and contingency, operating in the computer equipment industry, for a marketing management position on the West Coast with salary greater than $150K/year.

This search (in mid-2002) returned nine recruiters. To get the names of these recruiters, you would simply purchase them there online with a major credit card. This search would cost $9.00. Without spending the money to acquire the names, this tool still provides useful knowledge in planning your contact campaign, for you can determine how large or small the recruiter pool is for a particular specialty and geography.

ExecutiveAgent.com

ExecutiveAgent.com, another tool offered by Kennedy Information, takes the process one step beyond identifying recruiters–it also allows you to automatically launch contact with the recruiters you select. You can select recruiters using the same criteria as the advanced database search described above and indicate whether you are in a "passive" or "active" search. Then, in real time, you can deliver an electronic mailing to the select recruiter list. A resume is attached (Word documents or RTF, rich text format, documents are standard). You then customize the mailing with a compelling cover letter and subject line (see tips in next section). The electronic mailing would be from you, not ExecutiveAgent. Once you have completed these steps, the e-mailing is launched, and receipt confirmations are returned. Each search costs $99 at the time of this printing.

SearchSelect

Finally, Kennedy provides a software tool you can load and use on your own computer to bring home the selection and launch capabilities just

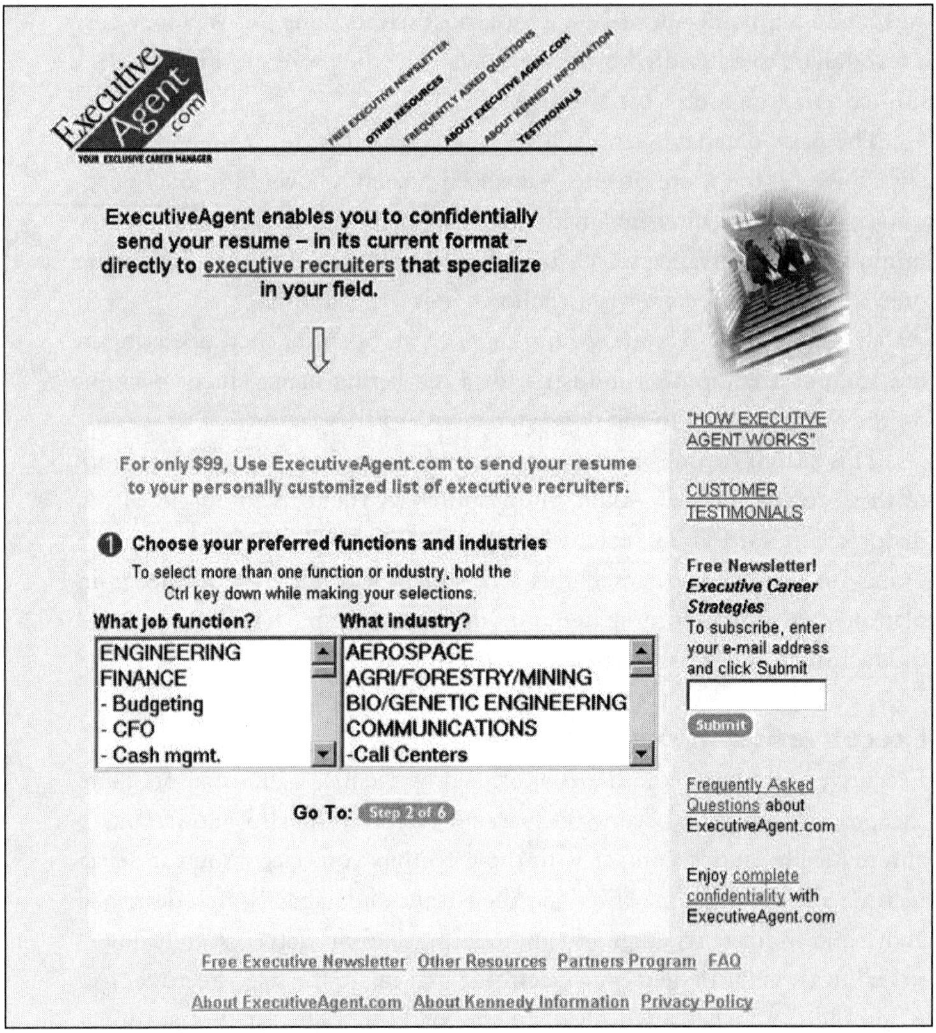

Figure 5.6. ExecutiveAgent.com

described in the Executive Recruiter Database and ExecutiveAgent. For $245 you can purchase the package ($195 if in conjunction with a Directory purchase) or obtain a one-year subscription with quarterly updates for $595.00. SearchSelect makes sense for extended campaigns, where individual searches and ExecutiveAgent campaign launch costs could add up. SearchSelect also affords the opportunity to automate a postal mail campaign with tools to print labels and envelopes. Other tools and educational resources are supplied in this package.

ExecutiveRegistry.com

Finally, in 2002, Kennedy Information introduced its flagship web-based career service, ExecutiveRegistry.com. Available to executives at the $100k+ salary-level, ExecutiveRegistry leverages the deep relationships that Kennedy Information has built with 15,000+ executive recruiters since it first published *The Directory of Executive Recruiters* in 1971.

ExecutiveRegistry gives career-minded professionals direct access to $100k+ positions and the recruiters that fill them. A 6-month membership starts at $179, and it gives members the opportunity to post their credentials, search a database of pre-screened executive-level jobs, and take advantage of a library of career tips. Because only qualified recruiters are permitted to post executive-level jobs and search for candidates, ExecutiveRegistry offers significantly more confidentiality than most other career sites. And, by posting their credentials, members can make themselves known to recruiters – including those that rarely advertise executive-level positions.

CONTACTING AND FOLLOWING UP WITH RECRUITERS

Once you select your target recruiters, you must build a campaign to contact them. There is no one right way to contact recruiters—each is different and each situation is different. Having the right materials, using the right methods, having the right expectations, and doing the right things to maintain the relationship are all important. Here are some basic tips from recruiters:

■ **Have a perfect resume and cover letter.** The resume and cover letter should be short and crisp, allowing the recruiter to know immediately your profile and expertise. No gimmicks—recruiters see through them and further—you don't want to "trick" the scanners many recruiters use to put resumes into databases. Chapter 8 covers these tools in greater detail.

■ Use regular mail and e-mail, and use e-mail with care.
Check with recruiters to verify if and how they want resumes sent. Call or
check Web sites. Mark materials as clearly as possible; "personal and confidential" always helps. If using e-mail, be aware that fear of viruses and
unsolicited dumps from resume mills may cause recruiters not to even open
unsolicited mail–unless the interest is clear from the subject. Janet Jones-
Parker of Jones-Parker/Starr advises to make the subject personal, specific,
credentialed and targeted: "Resume: John Smith IT executive looking for
CIO position" will get you further than simply "Resume."

■ Use the phone, but use it sparingly. It is never appropriate to
hound recruiters, but a brief follow-up phone call or two may help direct
attention to your resume and credentials. Recruiter opinions are divided on
this issue. Ms. Jones-Parker advises a short introductory phone call or
voicemail message after hours to advise that your resume has been sent, and
perhaps another phone call two weeks later to make sure it was received,
read and filed. Other recruiters advise to use phone calls sparingly or avoid
them altogether. In the words of Mark Jaffe, Wyatt & Jaffe Inc.: "Don't
park outside my window with a brass band. A gentle tap on the shoulder
will do."

■ Keep your file up-to-date. Presuming that they are either inac-
tive or inaccurate, recruiters routinely discard resumes after a few months.
It is a good idea to resubmit every four to six months. Some recruiters recommend follow-up phone calls stating your desire to keep your information updated and correct. If something changes about your credentials or
status, advise immediately. Chapter 7 goes deeper into how to work with
the recruiter on an ongoing basis.

**■ Don't expect acknowledgment, and don't take it personal-
ly if you don't get it.** Again, recruiters receive hundreds–thousands–of
them. No response simply means, in most cases, that there is no position
open that fits your qualifications. Again, remember, recruiters work for their
clients–not you–so their focus is on positions, not you as candidate.

With these tips in mind, the goal is to get an in-depth interview and
to start a working relationship. Chapter 7 explores strategies to make this
relationship most productive. In the mean time, Chapter 6 explains what

to do to make yourself more attractive to recruiters, how to get them to initiate the relationship, and what to do when they call you.

Depending on their business model and situation, recruiters may or may not be interested in your resume—they may wish to search and contact you instead. That said, it is still a good idea to plan a recruiter contact strategy, in which target recruiters are identified and contacted to build a working relationship. Kennedy Information provides a powerful set of tools to help select and contact specific recruiters.

Things a Headhunter Won't Tell You...

Ethical recruiters (and most are, by the way) recognize their responsibility to candidates as well as to the hiring organization and share as much information as possible about the position and the search process. Regrettably, however, sometimes communications break down because of neglect or nefariousness: you've got to be prepared for these eventualities as well.

Advice to Candidates

ITEM	EXPLANATION
We're quoting $150K, but they'll go to $200K if necessary.	You can't blame your new employer for wanting to get you for as small a compensation package as you feel comfortable accepting. Besides, this gives them more space for a raise if you perform well.
The last guy (person) in this job quit because he couldn't get along with the founder's son, who's the exec vp.	Blood is thicker than water, and nepotism is king at this place, but if you can stick it out for a few years and negotiate a fat contract, you'll still be ahead of the game.
You're the first candidate we're recommending here, mainly to test out our specs.	Somebody's got to be the walking horse, somebody's got to be first. Look at it this way: early bird gets the worm (sometimes).

ITEM	EXPLANATION
As a woman, you don't have much of a chance to get this job, but the client wants to be covered by EEO.	If it's any consolation to you, we're also throwing in a black and a guy with a limp.
The real reason we couldn't recommend you was those long sideburns and white socks.	Remember, this was for McKinsey & Co., not your everyday software house.
Too bad we didn't have a picture before calling you in for this interview.	Otherwise we'd have known you're a black female and would have gotten you in earlier in anticipation of scoring two points on our client's EEO scale.
You're perfect for the job, but I canyou as a source because we already have the search to find your company's new CEO.	Even headhunters follow only use the rules of the jungle.

CHAPTER 6
GETTING A RECRUITER TO FIND YOU

If you have the talent, and it's game day,
assume that a scout wll be there.
– Janet Jones-Parker, Jones-Parker/Starr

The very name "recruiter" itself implies that these professionals come and find you–not the other way around. Indeed, that's how it most often works, particularly in the higher levels of executive recruiting. In reality, the recruiter is being paid by the client company for two reasons: to find people and to bring them into its business. As such, especially for retained search firms, the business model is oriented towards true search, where the recruiter seeks out the candidates, works further with them to determine if they are a good prospect and then to "sell" them into making a transition.

So as a candidate, the sixty-four-dollar question is "If recruiters prefer to find me, and if many don't want to hear from me until they have a specific opening, how can I best position myself to be found? That's what this chapter is about.

WHO ARE RECRUITERS LOOKING FOR?

By now it should be clear that recruiters are looking for special "hard-to-find" individuals best suited for the client position. The retained search firm is looking for the best possible candidate and may settle for none at all if they do not fit the requirements or are not available. The contingency recruiter is looking for a good candidate but particularly a fast "match" to obtain compensation as quickly as possible. In either case, to make it happen they need to find well-differentiated candidates—those who stand out from the pack. Client firms don't hire recruiters to find "average" people.

Recruiters look for people who stand out in their profession—who represent state-of-the-art or best practice, who have made a contribution to their profession and shown leadership, who have exceeded expectations. Recruiters also look for people on an "upward trajectory" in their organizations. They are getting promoted, they are adding responsibility, and they are considered exceptional performers and leaders in their organizations. These attributes speak volumes. They also look for people on an upward trajectory in their field or industry—people who speak for and speak to the industry, publish papers and articles, and who are known authorities in their fields.

If this all sounds like you, you're in good shape and your phone has probably already been ringing from recruiters in your field. If it isn't quite you—or better yet, you think you possess some of these qualities but just haven't yet "gotten the word out," you're probably in good shape. There are many, many people in the professional workforce who do possess truly unique and differentiated talents—more than they think—but just haven't figured out how—or had the time—to bring them to light. Finally, if you really are "average," you can apply a little focus and commitment and become "above average." And, even if you haven't become an industry guru quite yet, you can take steps to build image and to bring yourself to light as a solid contributor.

HOW DO RECRUITERS FIND "EXCELLENCE"?

Recruiters can be among the most resourceful and creative of all business professionals. They can piece together facts, rumors, and anecdotal evidence to sniff out the best candidates from the darkest corners of almost any business. How do they do this? And how can you best fit their process? It might serve well here to review and add to the description of the "Executive Recruiter Process" in Chapter 4.

In a nutshell, recruiters rely on three things:

- External data and information sources

- The "network"
- Talent scouting skills

Taking each one at a time:

Finding Out Who's Who

Recruiters employ an array of public information resources to find people. We mentioned in Chapter 4 the use of annual reports and other pieces of public corporate record to identify the top two or three tiers of management in an organization. That's a good starting point, but frankly, anybody could do that, and those reports won't show who the up-and-comers are. Resourceful recruiters instead rely on a much broader assortment of available and less-available publications. They may also employ expensive subscription data services to get a closer look at companies, industries, and their key players. Here are a few of the widely used information sources:

- **Annual reports and other shareholder reports** provide top-level executive posts.
- **Subscription-based corporate information services,** such as Hoover's and Standard & Poor's provide not only up-to-the-minute corporate performance information but also complete press releases and detailed corporate profiles. These services cost plenty ($1000+/year) but help recruiters monitor the pulse of a business and the industry–and what the breakthroughs are and who is making them.
- **Major newspapers and magazines.** In general, *Business Week*, *Wall Street Journal*, *Forbes* and others are full of articles about people in business–but mostly the true cream of the crop.
- **Local newspapers and magazines** provide information on many more people at lower tiers in their organizations. Many of these papers have a careers section, where people on the move in their professions are called out. Recruiters will make note of these people and may put them into their database as placeholders for collecting more information.
- **Local business journals.** The Business Journal franchise (American City Business Journals, Inc.) has publications in about 70 cities or regions in the country. Each issue has a page or two of people and career transitions. Most recruiters will browse these publications, and in certain

specialties will keep a close eye on a select few. You can bet money that a North Carolina high-tech recruiter has access to the *San Jose Mercury News* (local daily newspaper) and the *San Jose Business Journal.*

- **Trade and industry association publications.** A recruiter specializing in marketing and advertising probably gets *Advertising Age*, and one specializing in transportation and logistics probably gets *Warehouse Management* and the *Journal of the American Production and Inventory Control Society.* You get the idea. And what are these recruiters looking for? They want to learn who's who in the industry and who the leaders and key contributors are. If you write an article, or if someone has written an article about you, that will get you a long way. Again, your name goes in the database, and the recruiter and his/her associates will tune in for more details–about you.

- **Trade and industry association events.** Almost every industry has one–and most have far more than one–national and regional forum where industry players get together to review the state-of-the-art in new techniques, products and services. Trade shows and events are designed to be marketing platforms for the exhibitors and buyers, but also educational events for industry participants of all types. Speakers are called in to present in breakout sessions in areas of their expertise. Industries and seminar companies catering to them hold educational symposiums where, again, guest speakers are sought after and brought in to explain some best practice in their industry. Upshot? If you can get asked to speak, you're putting yourself in a good position to be heard–by recruiters! Recruiters–particularly industry-focused recruiters–attend these events as baseball scouts attend baseball games. And they will get the mailing list to find out who's presenting. It's a great way for talented but obscure mid-level professionals to get their audition.

High-Speed Networking

Aside from the facts and other forms of tangible information acquired through publications and other media, every recruiter, without exception, has an active network of informants. Recruiters try to know people in the right places, so when the need comes up, they can get on the horn with their contact right away. These contacts can help identify good candidates–or other people who know good candidates. As recruiter Mark Jaffe says (see Chapter 4 headline quote), he believes he is "only two degrees of separation" from just about anyone. A few well-placed phone calls, and the savvy recruiter has a list of candidates–and a little scoop on each. Specialist recruiters may well know every possible candidate in their industry already–the network is used to find out who might be available.

You may find yourself to be–perhaps unwittingly–part of this network. You may contact, or be contacted by, a recruiter. Your hopes rise because now, you think, they're interested in you, and things will happen. But times goes on, and nothing happens! The recruiter has probably placed you in their network, and you may get calls looking for other candidates. If that happens, go with it. Cooperation is a good thing, and eventually it will be your turn. Recruiters genuinely appreciate this sort of cooperation, and in the course of it, you'll build a relationship, and they will get to know you better. None of this can hurt.

Talent Scouting

Many recruiters play the recruiting game much in the manner of a baseball scout. They get a promising lead. It may come from a journal article, promotion announcement, or a network connection. They may see a name in print, then call a buddy to get a little more information. If you're a dead-on prospect and the recruiter is working with an existing opening, you might get a call right then and there. But frequently, it's just a lead, just a little piece of information that says you're out there and you might have some of the right talent and skills. The recruiter will watch your ascent.

They may try to find out where you play next, and will get in line for tickets to size up your talents in person. It may be a seminar or a trade show. It may have nothing to do with your profession–it may be a local council or school board meeting. They will watch you, what you do (or have to say), and how you relate to others on the field. Do others respect you? Do they look at you as an authority? Do you handle questions well? Do you offer those rare qualities of solid, think-on-your-feet leadership? Do you understand the esoteric nuances of the business or environment you're in? Maybe you aren't the person they came to see, but they found you anyway. Many a good candidate is found this way. Can you start to see the value of exposure?

The above discussion is an overview of some of the vast assortment of techniques that recruiters use. There are others, and recruiters will each have their own mix of methods.

BUILDING YOUR PROFESSIONAL BRAND

You now know what recruiters do—now it's time to move on to discuss what you, as a candidate-to-be should do. Among the 50 million or so working professionals, how do you get noticed? Essentially, you are in charge of marketing yourself, and getting noticed means doing some good marketing. What does this mean? Bottom line—you must build yourself as a brand through positioning yourself well and creating visibility. In doing so you'll not only get on the radar screen, but you'll get there with a strong, clear image, compelling to the recruiter—and their clients.

What Is a Brand?

Marketers define a brand as a name, a series of attributes, and a reputation that create visibility and preference in the marketplace. "Tide" is a good detergent product technically. But the brand adds a name, a familiarity, an image, and a reputation that speaks far louder in the market than the underlying mix of chemical surfactants and builders. The brand name is worth as much or more than the product, and really, it is worth more than the name of the company (how big is the "Procter & Gamble" lettering on the box?). The brand defines the product.

In a similar way, you can build yourself as a "brand" in your company and industry, rising above the company you work for and the specific array of accomplishments (which may be technically good, but not entirely visible). Personal brand-building usually starts inside your own company. You get the big assignments, your name is on the tip of everyone's tongue as the expert and go-to person. You represent your firm in trade shows, seminars, college recruiting, and the like. You become the preferred mentor among all colleagues and younger employees. All along the way, you achieve on the job (don't forget that part!) Sooner or later, this leadership manifests itself in ever-higher positions in your company, even more visibility. You may not make it to Jack Welch status, but getting a name in your company, in your field, in your industry, in your niche will go a long way. To achieve this, you build your own brand, much as a company marketer tries to build a brand for their product.

How do you build your personal brand? Brand management is a combination of factors working together to build from the product itself into a reputation and visibility that sets it apart from other products on the shelf. Here are some tactics of the brand marketer, and how they might apply to you.

Quality Is Job One

A really good marketer can turn almost anything into a top seller. But for most products, a brand is built on intrinsic quality, customer satisfaction, and excellence of the product. This is also true for most employee/candidates. It is important to build on a base of performance. As an employee, you should achieve measurable, solid results above expectations. You must satisfy your internal and external customers and benefit your organization. You must do this consistently–not one-time flash-in-pan successes. The term "track record" is used to describe these attributes. Many people have more and better achievements than they realize–it is a good idea to take inventory and keep close track of your performance record–whether or not you're currently a candidate.

Distinguishable Characteristics

Good product fundamentals are important, but won't move the product off the shelves unless there are other distinguishing characteristics. Tide sold as a plain white sack of white powder probably would sell but wouldn't dominate its market nor would it be sought by customers. This is where positioning, image, packaging, and visibility all come in.

Take Your Position

Positioning is how marketers attempt to differentiate products. Here is where a series of "er" and "est" words come in: the highest quality, easiest, cheapest, fastest, cleanest, better-than-product-X kinds of statements come in. Products are positioned in the marketplace and among competitors. The same thought process can apply to you. Are you the best leader? The creative force? The best communicator? The best problem solver? The best program or project manager? The most well-rounded individual in your field, company or industry? You may not be the "most" of anything, but it's good to identify your strengths, capitalize on them, and promote them. Positioning yourself as your company's expert and best outside presenter in a field speaks volumes. Turnaround expert or morale builder or successful entrepreneur inside your company are all solid, credible positions. And yes, title can be important, too. While staying true and within your company guidelines, a "sexy" job title helps. It is a combination of deciding what you do best, doing it, and making it visible to the marketplace.

Elaborate, and elevate, but don't exaggerate. Marketing professionals will spin a product and a brand as much as possible, but they are careful not to stretch the product or brand promise too far. Hondas aren't performance cars and Coke isn't good for you no matter how marketed. And even if they, in fact, had these attributes, people wouldn't believe it anyway. The same goes in marketing yourself–don't stretch anything! Recruiters –and most employers–can see through it a mile away.

Think In and Out

Positioning and branding are important both inside and outside your business. As suggested earlier, it usually works best to establish your position internal to the company, then begin to take it outside. Turn a bad business into a good one–then make it known by speaking about it or writing about it publicly. If all goes well, recruiters will notice. Even if you aren't ready to change positions, once you establish a relationship with recruiters, it's a good idea to update them on your progress and accomplishments. There may be no response or acknowledgment from the recruiter at the time you advise them, but you can be sure they will track your progress, and when the time comes, they'll come for you. Of course, you don't want to send such an update weekly–only once in a while and only if the recruiter would obviously be interested. Such PR with recruiters must be done right, but it can go a long way.

Bring It to Market

At the end of the day, what makes Tide and all other brands work is image and visibility. The right package catches the customer's eye, and the right advertising, slogans, and reputation work together to create a favorable image. The ideal brand image campaign is a balanced approach. A series of TV soap opera ads with no other image enhancers–plain white boxes on the shelf–doesn't work as well, but it is still better than nothing.

Still, visibility in the corporate world can be tough to get. There are a lot of people out there looking for it, and there are only so many platforms on which to gain it. Further, a lot of what you do might be considered "company confidential"–you can't simply write an article describing your formula for adding 10 percent to your company's gross profit margin. But it should be obvious from the recruiter processes detailed that, if you get your name out there professionally, recruiters will find you. Here are some of the most effective ways to get publicity, both internal and external:

Get Known Inside Your Company

Reviewing why internal publicity is important: first, it leads to external publicity, and second, remember that recruiters network, and if you're known inside your company, you'll be easier to find. And how do you build your internal image? Achievement is probably the best way to become known, but there are ways you can highlight your achievements.

■ **Write articles.** Most companies have internal "organs"–publications highlighting accomplishments and individual achievements. It doesn't take too much to get into these. Remember, editors are always looking for good material. Some enterprising employees may even start their own intra-company newsletter (or even a Web page) describing what is going on in their job function. If you do this, keep in mind that quality and consistency of delivery are also important. It's embarrassing to write about a success one month, then have the project canceled or stop the newsletter the following month.

■ **Take on big projects.** If they're looking for someone to lead the worldwide customer satisfaction program, take it on! Volunteerism means hard work but also leads to visibility and an ever-more-rapid escalation of your stock among peers. Eventually, these achievements will get outside, whether through the network or a more direct spotlight on what you're doing.

■ **Speak.** Speaking clearly works outside the organization, but it also works inside. Build that traveling road show for your department and take it around the world or to the sales force. Represent your group in important strategy-setting meetings or customer visits. Unless you're a particularly poor speaker, the visibility gained will be well worth the effort. And the speech delivered internally is good practice for the speech delivered outside.

■ **Hold conferences and meetings.** A great way to gain visibility and show leadership is to offer to host or hold meetings to resolve important issues or design major strategic breakthroughs. Most of the time, your colleagues or managers will appreciate your going above and beyond to do this, and the reputation you'll get as leader, organizer and solver will do great things for your brand.

And, Get Known to the World

Getting noticed means making yourself noticeable. Sounds like common sense, but many competent professionals lay around in wait for their break. Bad practice. If you get lucky or are particularly good, it might happen that way. But more likely, if you take a passive approach, the opportunities for external publicity will go to someone else. It is a good idea to take the initiative. If you do, you may find it isn't really that hard. Just as magazine and newspaper editors are always hungry for material, so too are meeting planners, seminar leaders, associations, and other venues hungry for material and leadership. If you have something to offer, you'll get the chance. It doesn't have to be breakthrough rocket science. Sharing even small but differentiated successes—or even the successful application of an industry best practice—will often get you there. And in some venues, all you need to do is make the effort. Here are some of the ways to get external visibility:

■ **Be active in industry or trade associations.** Participate actively, or better yet, take leadership positions, in these organizations. Networking opportunities abound, and recruiters read Web sites and printed material with your name on it. If you host meetings, find extraordinary speakers, speak yourself, edit or help with the newsletter, and go outside to find other excellence. Sooner or later this effort will come back to help you. Attend trade shows and organization events. Represent your company and staff your booth. Write papers, build knowledge and research. There are a hundred ways to participate and contribute.

- **Speak.** It works internally, and it works even better externally. Offer to speak at seminars. You usually won't get paid, but if you do, so much the better. You should get free travel. Seminar and meeting leaders are always looking for material. Doing such a presentation works wonders in many dimensions. First, anytime you have to present a body of knowledge to an unfamiliar audience, you get better at presenting it and what is important about it. It helps to coalesce your knowledge and expertise. External publicity begets internal publicity. The word that you presented a paper at the industry conference gets around. More importantly, from a recruiting standpoint, recruiters, particularly specialists, know who is talking from following the industry. Seeing your name, they will attempt to learn more about you and may even try to see you or meet you in person.

- **Write articles.** Writing articles works much the same as speaking. You get a chance to gel your thoughts and accomplishments into reader-friendly form, and your name and accomplishments get out there for the world—and recruiters—to see. Even career announcements, which may seem trivial to you, can get you noticed. And if you can get someone to write an article about you, so much the better. Even if the article stops short of what you yourself would have done, a third-party endorsement often does a lot for your image.

- **Be active in your community.** Community activity is evidence of leadership and effort beyond the normal course of duty, and it too provides good opportunities for networking. Getting involved in local government, civic organizations, arts communities, charities and the like can be well worth your time if you're trying to build your brand for recruiters. And don't forget your college community—staying active with alumni associations and keeping the alumni newsletter updated with your career moves can get you spotted by recruiters—particularly if they went to your school.

WHAT TO DO WHEN THE RECRUITER CALLS YOU

So you did everything right up to this point. You've achieved and made yourself visible. The phone rings at 4:30 in the afternoon, and it's Tom Headhunter, dropping upon you a tempting position that's a "must" career move; you'll be glad you did it. At the end of 10 minutes of talk, little is known of the position, and nothing is known of Tom Headhunter. What do you do? How do you decide if this position—and this person—are worth doing business with?

It's hard, because you don't want to be taken for a ride into a vast unknown, risking your confidentiality and relationship with your current employer—and perhaps other recruiters. Just the same, you don't want to hastily turn M. Headhunter aside. There may be some value in the position and the potential relationship. When these cold calls come in, most recruiters advise the following:

First Things First–Interview the Recruiter

It may sound like an odd way to turn the tables, but it's probably good to start with a few qualifying questions to Mr. Headhunter before moving on. Find out:

■ **Who they are, what firm they represent.** A recruiter should disclose his/her firm and whether it's a contingency or retainer firm. If they won't do this, you should be skeptical. Don't necessarily expect them to identify the client (hiring) firm, however. If they do, that's great, but often they won't and they've been instructed not to.

■ **Background in field.** Ask the recruiter how long they have been in their firm and industry, what types of placements they've made, what kinds of clients they have. Specific names are better, but you may not get them. Just as the recruiter will want to know more about you, you should know more about them before proceeding. If they appear to be a competent, experienced professional in the field for which they recruit, that's good. If they are a used car salesman trying to pry you loose for something so they can get a quick commission, that's bad.

■ **Learn their process.** Ask a few questions about how they conduct business. From reading this book, you should have a good idea of how the recruiting process should work.

Don't Commit to Anything

It's never a good idea to go too far down the path in the first call. Yes, a recruiter's time is important, and if it's one of the industry top names on the phone, it might be in your best interest to keep going. But for Tom Headhunter, it's good to get some information, start the relationship, and then step aside. "I'll get back to you" is a good line to keep in mind.

What do you do before getting back to Tom?

1. First, think through everything that was said. Does the position really sound like a fit for your experiences and objectives? Most people get excited, even emotional, at the prospect of somebody wanting them. You must let this emotion subside and find out whether you really want to be wanted in the situation. At the risk of a tenuous analogy, think through your dating experiences.

2. Do your own research. Look up the recruiter in Kennedy Information's *Directory of Executive Recruiters*. Is it a reputable firm? Does it indeed specialize in your industry? Has it been around for a while, and is it a member of AESC or other accrediting organizations? Look at its Web site. What types of positions does it deal with? What type of clients, if it discloses? Does the site and its message have a professional tone and manner, or is it salesy?

3. Then, use your network. Talk to peers, colleagues and recruiters if you know any. Talk to people outside your organization but in your industry. Have they heard of or dealt with Tom Headhunter and/or his firm? Do they know what kind of clients this recruiter typically works with?

After satisfying yourself with these answers, call the recruiter back. It may take you minutes or days to get comfortable, but getting comfortable is important. Whether you initiate a recruiter relationship this way or by contacting the recruiter initially, the next step is to work with that recruiter towards a productive and effective job placement.

CHAPTER 7
GETTING RESULTS: HOW TO WORK
EFFECTIVELY WITH A RECRUITER

The simplesst thing to remember is less is more.
– Mark Jaffe, Wyatt & Jaffe

You've made the connection. You successfully made yourself known to a recruiter, either through networking or direct contact. Or, a recruiter has found you. Either way, you now have a relationship. Like any relationship, if nurtured and nourished, it will prosper. If neglected or abused, it will turn to dust. Obviously, beginning the relationship with a recruiter is an important step towards achieving your career transition goal. But you must do the right things along the way to make that relationship productive. Otherwise, you'll alienate the recruiter and have problems connecting with the hiring client.

This chapter brings out the do's and don'ts of working with an executive recruiter once the relationship has begun. The three areas central to the discussion are attitude, protocol, and tools. Attitude refers to your own approach to the recruiter relationship and your expectations of it. Protocol refers to how you interact with the recruiter and client firm, and tools refer to the things you bring to the relationship–resumes, cover letters, references and interviewing skills. The right combination of attitude, protocol and tools will help you land a job most efficiently, preserve the greatest number of options, and navigate the tricky waters of issues such as confidentiality with your current employer.

ATTITUDE IS EVERYTHING
Once again, a quick regression back to the world of dating relationships provides the right backdrop for starting a recruiter rela-

tionship. As a dating relationship unfolds, does it work to approach it with a negative attitude and an endless series of lies designed to unduly impress? The bad attitude part works for about five minutes, and lies get undressed shortly thereafter. It really works the same way in a recruiter relationship. How you approach the relationship from the very beginning has a lot to do with how it turns out. You need to have the right expectations, the right attitude, the right persona, and the right preparation at the outset.

The First Few Minutes

It is likely that your first contact with a recruiter will be by phone, unless you're spotted at a trade show or some other gathering or are introduced through networking. And if you're a senior executive, that first phone call is likely to be followed quickly by a short in-person interview. In any event, the first impressions are extremely important. What are these recruiters doing in these early stages? They are checking you out, personally and professionally. They do this very efficiently. Who are you, what do you have to say, and how well do you say it? Are you who you say you are, and how well do you carry yourself? Do you have charisma and leadership skill? Mark Jaffe of Wyatt & Jaffe offers: "There is something to be said about the clairvoyant powers of an executive recruiter. They can size up someone in about a minute and a half."

What does this mean? You should be prepared and professional from the start. Don't assume that you'll get to the important stuff later. You must be sharp, helpful, honest, and to the point from the beginning. It is a business relationship—and it needs to start, continue and finish that way.

Honesty Is (Still) the Best Policy

As the ancient saying goes: "Above all, be thyself." It is very important to present an accurate and honest picture of yourself and your accomplishments. Recruiters and their clients know that no candidate is perfect—it is acceptable to have a few warts and "career mulligans" on your resume. In fact, if you don't, you may create a few suspicions you didn't expect! Recruiters can smell resume "stretch" a mile away. Resumes and all of your communications should reflect sort of a modest confidence (and we'll talk about in a minute). Inflating accomplishments, responsibilities and job titles soon becomes self-evident. Credibility is extremely important, and showing some of the "bad stuff" and being able to explain why it was bad will build more credibility than a perfect resume. (Chapter 8 covers resumes in greater detail.)

Keep the Glass Half Full

Angry at your last boss? Discontent with your current company's business practices or strategy? Not content with your career path? Recruiters advise you to bottle up these feelings and keep them away from recruiter (and client) interaction. Too often, these negativisms come up, almost as a way to justify your career transition. Venting your frustrations will get the recruiter–and maybe your employer–on your side, right? Not really. Recruiters see it differently. Negative barbs about your previous position can raise yellow flags. There may be something in your background or something bad that happened that you're not talking about. Moreover, clients are looking for loyal employees, and if you're beating up your current firm and current boss, you may look like a disloyal, high-maintenance nightmare to be avoided.

Remember–there's always the chance your criticism could make it back to the wrong ears–your employer's ears–during your search. The negative consequences are obvious. Much better is to spread a positive message–not only for the benefit of your recruiter and future employers, but also, just in case it circles back to where you are.

But you don't want to cover your current position and company with flowers. The best approach is to be objective. If there are problems at your previous employer, you can talk about them–but as a businessperson, not as a disgruntled employee. Recruiters and their clients may want to hear your analysis of a previous situation and may appreciate your prescient understanding of and solutions for the situation. But as a general rule, don't go there unless it's relevant to the discussion, and in the words of recruiter Smooch Reynolds: If you must vent, do it with family members."

Expect the Right Things

As with any relationship, if you expect the right things from the outset, things will go much better.

It is worth reinforcing the point that the recruiter's customer is the client hiring firm–not you. To resurrect the earlier analogy, you are the product, and the recruiter is working to market you to that customer. This can't and won't work if you don't cooperate, and it is only in the rarest of circumstances that you can turn the relationship around and become a demanding customer requiring satisfaction. If your name isn't Jack Welch or Lou Gerstner, we wouldn't recommend trying it.

It's a good idea in the beginning to convey to the recruiter that you understand the relationship, their role and your role. That puts you on the right foot, and a recruiter is more willing to work with you if you understand the process. It shows that you've done your homework, and recruiters like working with people who have done their homework.

Although the recruiter is working directly for the client company, you should also expect that they will have an interest in you if what you offer fits client needs. If you are a good fit for the position, they will work with you and move the process forward. No amount of active communication or selling on your part will get them to do otherwise. If you approach the relationship with this idea and communicate with recruiters when you have something to add to your background that might fit somebody's needs, that will work. Those "anything new?" phone calls to the recruiter usually don't work. Assume that the recruiter has you in mind–at least in back of mind if not top of mind–and contact the recruiter when you have something to add to the "product." Otherwise, it's best to let the recruiter drive and take you to where they best think you need to go. Don't expect a lot of handholding, immediate response to phone calls or acknowledgment. Some recruiters may give career and tool advice, but others may not. You should establish this in the beginning.

Finally, you should give the process time. Be patient. Executive placements often take three or four months unless you're a perfect match right off the bat. Some higher-level executive placements take up to a year.

Quiet Confidence

Much as in life in general, an understated, dignified approach to a job search and a recruiting relationship will get you further. If you position yourself as good at what you do and confident in your qualities, people will come to you. If you come off as brash, conceited and arrogant, people turn the other way. In the world of job search, it's a fine line between confidence and arrogance. Employers look for confidence, and they look for take-charge people who can lead and get things done. The personality qualities that achieve this result, if left unchecked, can often lead to arrogant, know-it-all behavior. Yes, you do want to market your capabilities and brag just a little. But keep it leashed, understated, tasteful, and truthful. "Act as if you had it made," according to Mark Jaffe, but don't "toot your own horn." "Be egotistical in a modest sort of way," said Gardner Heidrick of Heidrick and Struggles.

The other side of this coin is not being confident enough or proud enough of your achievements. It is always important to take inventory of your achievements, your responsibilities, and what others think and say of you. People with arrogant personalities tend to do too little self-assessment, which leads to overstating what they do know about themselves, while people with modest personalities tend to underestimate their case. Thus the first step towards a dignified, confident approach is to be fully aware of your attributes and qualities.

Be Willing to Help

Recruiters best help those that help themselves. But they also best help those who help them. It starts with providing the right information and updates. Further, it helps the recruiter to be objective in evaluating positions. Don't accept an interview if it really doesn't interest you. And if the recruiter needs a referral–be willing to help. Your turn will come.

Err On the Side of Formality

It's sometimes hard to tell how casual and friendly–or formal and businesslike–a recruiter wants to be. Every recruiter is different, and for that matter, client firms are different too–according to industry, location, type of position, and individual personalities involved. The best advice is to err on the side of formality. You shouldn't treat a recruiter like your best friend. Dress a little better than you think you otherwise might need to. Use formal business letters, not scribbles on post-it notes. Use formal, objective language when talking to recruiters. If the conversation transitions to jokes and slang at the recruiter's lead, you can follow—but don't assume it will do so. Recruiters want to see your businesslike demeanor, even if it isn't absolutely necessary to your direct interaction with them.

Prepare Thy Recruiter

Without overburdening the recruiter with detail, you want to give a complete picture of your professional life and a good look at your external life and contacts in addition. You are a person and a professional, and the recruiter needs to see the whole picture. Your resume documents your professional life, and a combination of your resume, references, cover letters, and your own self-appraisal will paint the more complete picture of both your professional and personal life. Make sure the recruiter has as much as possible—a complete resume, a list of references, a few anecdotes from these references, and a few short sound bytes from you about you. These should be presented in neat, organized form, as in a professional presentation you might do for a higher-level manager or a client or customer. If you provide a recruiter more than five or six pages total about you, that's probably too much. The recruiter won't remember it all, but should know what's there and where to get it. The next section goes deeper into the tools of the recruiter relationship—all an important part of the preparation imperative.

THE RIGHT TOOLS

Like any project, it always helps to have the right tools and preparation available. A recruiter cannot be expected to approach a client effectively without at least a base portfolio of material about you. You can't present a product or a project on your job without some degree of preparation, and better yet, proper visual aids. Similarly, it is hard for a recruiter to present you without such material. Recruiters should be adequately prepared with your resume, a cover letter, salary history, a set of references, and the knowledge that you're prepared for an interview.

The Resume

The art and science of resume writing has been covered in detail in dozens of other works, and is covered in depth in Chapter 8 of this book. The resume needs not only to reflect your history and accomplishments, but it also must convey your skills and attributes—that is—how everything fits together to build your professional profile. In one page (maybe one and a half or two, for an experienced player) the recruiter and client should get a pretty clear picture of who you are and what you've done. Resumes can be functional or chronological:

- Functional resumes identify your skills and competencies and organize information and examples to support those skills.
- Chronological resumes describe your experiences starting from most recent and working backwards.

Resumes should go beyond being just a laundry list of experiences. Good resumes paint a clear picture of what you can do, how you are perceived, and how fast you're moving in the organization. They should reflect the kinds of assignments you've received, their importance, and how well you've performed them. They should convey the attributes of job performance—technical competence, versatility, creativity, judgment, and leadership. Finally, resumes need to be brief, to the point summaries designed to capture interest. Remember that they lead to the interview—not directly to the job.

Remember also, resumes should be kept completely up-to-date. An out-of-date resume causes embarrassing situations and raises suspicions. As pertinent new information becomes available, it's a good opportunity for dialogue with the recruiter.

The Cover Letter

Cover letters go with a resume and are used in varying ways by recruiters. With a cover letter, you introduce yourself, summarize your qualifications, and try to "hook" the reader to read your resume and go further. Recruiters may or may not use cover letters in their presentation to clients. Cover letters may be standard or customized for each position and company approached. Recruiters, particularly high-end recruiters, recommend very short, quiet, confident cover letters—perhaps as few as three lines. As Jaffe says, "Less is more." Again, there is more on cover letters in Chapter 8.

Your References, Please

References are very important in the executive recruiting process. Recruiters will use references to further screen and evaluate you towards defining their candidate panel for clients. If you navigate the selection process successfully and the client is considering making an offer, the client will put your references into play once again. Thus, building a list of references is important from the beginning.

Reference lists should be carefully considered and constructed. Reference lists that omit or bias coverage can be harmful. A good reference list has at least four or five professional references on a managerial or supervisory level from your company or industry and a few personal references as well.

Whether or not to include references from your current employer can be a troublesome question, for contact may well "blow your cover" as you search for a new position. Some recommend using a mentor or close personal associate in your company as a reference instead of your direct manager.

References should, of course, be advised that they are being used as references. It can be helpful to have a few of your key references prepare a short written summary of their experience and perception of you as a professional–particularly if confidentiality is an issue. These can be done blind–you don't want a manager from a competing firm calling your manager to talk about you. Reference lists should furnish, for each reference, their name, title, company, your relationship with them, how long you've known them or worked with them, and contact information. If it comes up, you should give authority to contact anyone on your reference list.

Salary History

It may seem like jumping the gun to give a recruiter your salary history before getting through a selection and interview process, but most recruiters recommend making this available. First, it gives another dimension to your overall track record. If you are landing 20 percent annual increases in a 3 percent inflation environment, you must be doing something right. And people in the market for something generally don't talk too long before getting to price–a client may want to know what you "go for" at an early stage in the process. They too may use your salary as a qualifier. If they are searching for what they estimate to be a $150K/year position, and you made $68K last year, you probably don't qualify, without going further. Likewise, if you made $300K last year, they may come to a similar "mismatch" conclusion. Be sure to supply non-cash compensation, such as bonuses, stock options, perks, and deferred compensation.

Getting Ready for the Interview

Like resumes and resume writing, the interview process has been thoroughly analyzed and covered in a variety of career management media. You've probably been exposed to the standard interview questions time and time again. "Where do you see yourself in five years?" "Why are you seeking this position?" and "Tell us why you're a good fit for this position." Over the years–particularly at senior management levels–there has been a shift away from the standard process towards what's referred to as "behavioral" interviewing. Why? Because the line of questioning was becoming so standardized that people could almost memorize answers. Interviewing became almost a form of play-acting in which a candidate could build and rehearse a script, nail the interview, and land a job for which they might not have been qualified.

So what is "behavioral" interviewing? In behavioral interviewing, the interviewer asks how you would respond to certain situations. They might present a situation, or even a case, and ask how you would deal with it. In so doing, they are not only testing your knowledge, experience, and skill, but also your ability to think on your feet to prepare and deliver answers. Another trend on the interview front is panel interviews in which you interview not with one but a whole team from the hiring client. These interviews are less structured and more realistic–more like a real business situation–than a traditional interview, and broad range of topics will be covered at once. (You can't prepare to speak finance with the finance person, then marketing with the marketing person. They are all there at once and your answers will have to satisfy all at once!)

Upshot: preparing for interviews these days means sharpening your knowledge and having a thorough understanding of your skills. You can't prepare a script, but should be prepared to apply your skills and knowledge to whatever the client may throw at you. And naturally, the more you know about the client in advance, the better you will do this. It boils down to having a clear-eyed view of how to apply your background and skills in business situations and knowing as much as you can about your client before the interview.

THE RIGHT PROTOCOL

You've established the relationship and furnished the recruiter with all the information they need. Now what? Just sit on your thumbs and wait for the phone to ring? In a way, yes. The proverbial ball is in the recruiter's court, but you need to be prepared for that unexpected hard baseline return volley. It is important to maintain proper communication with the recruiter and to properly engage with the recruiter and client firm for the interview.

Communication: Not Too Little, Not Too Much

Many a recruiter relationship has been spoiled by over-communication. That weekly "Have you found anything yet?" call is unproductive at best and is usually counterproductive. Recruiters don't like to be hounded. As Bill Kelly of Kelly & Company puts it: "Leave me alone—but you need to stay on the radar screen." Yes, this implies a delicate balance. Here are a few tips and pointers:

- **Set protocol in the beginning.** Once a recruiter accepts your credentials and shows interest in working with you, discuss how and how often you will touch base.
- **Trust the recruiter.** Have faith that the recruiter remembers you and your needs. Remember, you are key to their process, too.
- **Be polite and patient with everyone.** You may get calls from researchers and associates in the recruiter's business. Treat them as professionals.
- **Don't call just for updates.** It isn't productive to call just for the latest. Wait for the recruiter to call you, or if you do call the recruiter, make sure there is substance and value—something to add to your portfolio or to the search.
- **Don't expect acknowledgment.** Recruiters are busy, and no news should generally be construed as good news.

■ **Don't contact employers directly.** Let recruiters work the process.

In general, you should treat the recruiter relationship as any other business relationship. Communicate when communication is needed, use communication to supply information and facts, and stick within a process that's established and comfortable for both of you.

Handling the Interview

If all goes well, sooner or later you will be called in for an interview with an employer. There is an extensive amount of preparation and protocol required in the interview process itself (prepare, dress properly, show up early, and so forth). The detail is again beyond the scope here and is the subject of a variety of books and treatments. What's important here is how to

---

15 Tips to Working With Recruiters

To summarize the material covered to this point, James Kennedy, founder of Kennedy Information, offers these 13 tips to keep in mind as you work with recruiters:

1. Have a clear career game plan and job-changing mindset.

2. Be open but cautious.

3. Ask questions to help determine the recruiter's legitimacy, credibility, reputation, and modus operandi. Find out if they are contingency or retainer, exclusive assignment or not, what professional affiliations they have, and what location they're from.

4. Never stretch the truth about job experience, education, income, etc.

5. Bow out early if you're really not interested: offer to be a resource if not a candidate.

6. Do you homework on the client organization once identified (the recruiter should provide basic material such as the annual report, but go beyond to clippings, trade publication articles, etc.

7. Don't play hard to get. Keep appointments, return calls, and cooperate.

8. Sign the reference-checking authorization if presented: it proves you have nothing to hide.

9. Cover yourself at work: despite all precautions and confidentiality, slip-ups some-work with the recruiter in the interview process. Again, tips and pointers:

■ **Let the recruiter work for you.** Have the recruiter set everything up and introduce you. You should not contact the client firm directly, unless you're three blocks away and lost.

■ **Keep your schedule open and flexible.** Time is of the essence for the client and the recruiter. Be responsive, return phone calls, and keep appointments.

■ **If it isn't right, graciously decline the interview.** Don't feel you have to please a recruiter or go through an interview just to stay on board. If the job is on Alaska's North Slope, and you just don't want to move your family there, say so. If you're not ready to move across the country for a wholly lateral career move, say that, too. It's good to advise the recruiter why you declined to help the recruiter learn what situations to avoid.

---

times occur. Tell superiors you're always getting calls from recruiters, but that doesn't mean you're looking.

10. Don't cultivate an offer just to get leverage where you are: such short term, self-serving strategy usually backfires.

11. Of 200 "suspects" uncovered in initial research, perhaps 50 will make the first cut, 5 will be finalists, and one will get the job. Don't take it personally: the search process aims for a perfect fit (particularly retained search), and it's probably in your best interests anyway.

12. Don't burn your bridges with the recruiter or your present employer

13. Let the recruiter run interference for you: on salary and benefits and perks. While compensated by the hiring organization, the search consultant can be your advocate, too, and has a stake in your success.

14. Make sure you take the recruiter's call after you get the job. Or, the next time you're on the beach, he won't return your calls either!

15. Remember that the recruiter is paid by the other side and is only interested in you if you can be converted into a bank deposit. don't expect him or her to return you calls or give you an interview (but expose yourself to enough reruiters and you'll get some action.)

Source: James H. Kennedy, founder and former editor of *Executive Recruiter News*

- **Let the recruiter help you prepare.** The recruiter should tell you something about the position, the type of hiring firm, and the interviewing manager or manager panel. They may not be able to tell you who the company is–directly–nor a lot of detail about the job, but trust that they will tell you what they can. The more you can know going in, the better.

- **Debrief the recruiter when done.** Give the recruiter an executive summary of what happened in the interview, whom you talked to, what you talked about, what went well and what didn't. The recruiter will be in touch with the employer again, and if there are additional issues, the recruiter can help resolve them. The recruiter who is better prepared to work with the client will be more effective. Likewise, you may get good feedback yourself.

- **Let the recruiter furnish your references.** Your discussion with the client should be about you. The recruiter will handle the other details.

- **Let the recruiter handle dialogue and negotiation.** Again, normally don't contact the client firm directly. The recruiter (particularly a retained search firm) knows the client and can play an instrumental role in resolving details of an offer. You don't want to get into a tough negotiation with someone who might be your future boss. However, you should stick up for your interests and not accept an offer too low. Although the recruiter is working for the client–and it seems they might put the hiring firm's interest ahead of yours–this is uncommon. The are usually trying to find a "win-win," both satisfying the client and meeting your needs. Otherwise, the placement won't work in the long run even if it does off the bat. You can help by making it clear to the recruiter what you want.

A good recruiter relationship is generally a long-term relationship, even if a job placement happens quickly. It is in your best interests as a candidate, both for your current job and for any future job, to work well with a recruiter. The best approach is to treat them as a business partner, as a working channel for your skills and talents, and to let them deal with the customers and do the merchandising.

Chapter 8 will explore the resume and cover letter tools in greater depth, then Chapter 9 will cover the "endgame"–the details of the job offer, acceptance, and what happens after that.

CHAPTER 8
GETTING THE WORD OUT

Half the money I spend on advertising is wasted;
the problem is, I don't know which half.
– David Olgivy

o matter how long you have been in the workforce or how many jobs you have held, it seems that swriting a resume never gets any easier. You could be a career professional for 20 years and still find yourself asking the same questions you did when you applied for your very first job: How many pages? Do I include references? Should I order it chronologically or functionally?

Add to this confusion the more recent issues of job-hopping and the necessity of ever-increasing computer and software skills, and resume writing can become a truly confounding experience. This chapter explores specific resume and cover letter strategies and some of the latest trends in how these devices are used.

WHAT IS A RESUME FOR?

Writing a resume is difficult because you may feel pressured to try and sum up your entire working life on one or two sheets of paper. But consider the resume's purpose and whom it is for. These days, it is not, as most think, a linear description of your career life and skills, a well-written summary of your professional accomplishments. Nor are you the one who will be reading it. Rather, a resume serves to do one thing:

Get you a job.

Or in the case of the recruiter, to get them to call you–and get you a job. If they don't like your resume, they won't try to match you to available positions, and your credentials and background won't see the light of day at hiring firms.

Getting you a job is the important thing–not what font to use or where to list your education. That's it, nothing more. Keep that concept in mind as you go along, separating the fluff from the essential, and you will find writing your resume a much smoother process.

BEFORE YOU BEGIN

Before you start typing, you should get yourself in the right mindset. The resume that gets results in the executive recruiting world today may be very different from what you have had in the past. You need to have impact and stand out, yet you want to exude a quiet, genuine confidence that draws the recruiter and employer to want to find out more. Consider the wisdom offered by from Mark Jaffe of retained search firm Wyatt & Jaffe:

■**Think of your resume as a first date.** You don't want to tell your date every detail of every relationship you have ever had on the first date. Contrary to what you've been taught before, don't include every job, every task on your resume, and don't worry about accounting for employment gaps yet. Put only information relevant to the job you want. Make it pithy, concise, short on words and deep on meaning. Every piece of information on your resume is something that can help you or hurt you; emphasize that which can help you.

■**Have a little attitude.** You want your resume to say, "Here I am, come and get me." Start now thinking of yourself as a professional deserving of a great position, and it will show in your resume. Don't be afraid to brag; this is your chance to showcase your accomplishments. Make sure they are on the resume. On the other hand...

■**Don't use self-descriptive fluff.** It's like a guy in a cheap polyester suit. The more plaid, the more gold chains, the more you wonder what he's trying to hide. Use only specific, action-oriented words that describe accomplishments ("produced" or "streamlined"), not words like "visionary" or "strong communication skills."

■**The heart of the matter.** "Show me your strengths right off the bat," says Jaffe. "Don't make me turn to the second page to get to the heart of what you are." Get your most important accomplishments at the top of your resume, even if they are chronologically out of order. You want to show exactly what you have done in your career, not describe your personality.

A SAMPLE RESUME

As in most things, a picture or example is worth a thousand words of description. The resume on the following pages (Figure 8.1) is offered as an example for discussion:

The sample resume format is the type that is preferred today by retained search firms. Note its simple construction and narrative format. Its "Expertise" section is a no-nonsense summary of defined accomplishments. "Experience" uses only year dates (not months) and has quantifiable amounts of improvement (4X, 25% increase). Overall, the resume has specific achievements but also a detached feel to it–almost an attitude – as if to say "I know I'm good–should we talk?"

FREQUENTLY ASKED QUESTIONS

It is helpful to address the 15 most common questions people have about writing resumes at any level in their career.

How Many Pages Should My Resume Be?

There is no definitive answer to this classic resume question. For those new to the workforce, one page will do, but it can be two. After 10-20 years in a career, three or even four pages may be in order, although short, crisp resumes are still more likely to be read. As long as your experience is worthy and presented in a concise manner, no recruiter is going to toss your resume in the trash simply because it's more than one page. It isn't so much the length but rather the content – just exercise good judgment.

Should I Include All of My Past Jobs?

This depends on the length of your career. If you are a college student, you will want to include the summer you interned at your dad's law firm, but

Jennifer Dawn Hayes
1414 Old Brownsville Road
Bartlett, TN 38134
901-555-1328
jdhayes@hayes.com

EXPERTISE

Executive-level technology and operating leadership, from product definition to P & L management, including full organizational control of strategic planning, market planning, R & D, technology development, manufacturing, human resources, business alliances and related corporate initiatives. Extensive turn-around and revitalization experience. Special emphasis on data storage and other peripheral products.

EXPERIENCE

1996 to Present   ACME SYSTEMS   San Francisco, CA

President and Chief Operating Officer

Introduced a state-of-the-art line of solid imaging office products for this $100M innovator of rapid prototyping equipment. Designed, implemented reorganization of development process and teams resulting in four major new platforms, including a high-end product with 4X throughput and quality at a lower cost. Improved factory cycle times by five fold. Enhanced performance of European and Asian sales teams.

1994 to 1996   MAXIMUM CORPORATION   Denver, CO

General Manager, EVP and Member of the Board

Initiated a major focus on time-to-market, development methodology and new product introduction for this $1.2B manufacturer of magnetic recording disk drives, taking the company from last-to-market to tied for first within 15 months. Engineered a restructuring of all operations except finance, including a manufacturing process which reduced the number of operators required for product build from 50 to 7. Introduced a new electronics architecture, reducing board cost by 25% while doubling performance.

1992 to 1994   MAGNETICS INCORPORATED   Sacramento, CA

President and Chief Operating Officer

Increased manufacturing capabilities of thin film head production nearly six fold for this $350M maker of magnetic recording components, directing the thin film head group toward high performance products. Built state-of-the-art wafer fabrication facility, on the largest wafer size in the industry, at that time. Technology focus was on novel thin film head sensors, magnetoresistive heads and advance slider designs and processes.

Figure 8.1. Sample Executive Resume

Page Two

| 1990 to 1992 | NATIONAL STORAGE INCORPORATED | Memphis, TN |

Executive Director and Co-Founder

Created the first multi-company storage industry research and development group, consisting of 15 corporate sponsors and more than a dozen university affiliates. The goal was to foster joint cooperative research activity. NSI received one of the first Advanced Technology Program (ATP) awards from the Department of Commerce (only 11 out of 250 submissions awarded). NSI has received over $100M in federal matching funds during the last 5 years.

| 1988 to 1992 | SUPREME STORAGE SYSTEMS | San Jose, CA |

Division Director

Directed technology development and manufacturing for all mid-range and high-end storage subsystems at this $4B business unit, including particulate and thin film media, thin film and MR recording heads, and advance channels. Ran facilities in both San Jose and Mainz, Germany. Later directed fixed disk file development in San Jose, Rochester, MN and Havant, England, including drives for high-end PC applications through mainframe systems. Successfully introduced several unique products such as the first drives with MR heads, parallel headed-high data rate drives, hot pluggable main-frame systems and new RAID configurations, among others.

| 1983 to 1988 | GENERAL PRODUCTS COMPANY | San Jose, CA |

Managed various technology groups in both product development and manufacturing, chiefly involving magnetic recording, optical recording and tape storage, including materials, mechanics and electrical engineering, and physics.

| 1975 to 1983 | IBM – RESEARCH DIVISION | San Jose, CA |

Managed and participated in technology groups for optical recording, xerography, lasers, optics, high-temperature elastomers, lithography, and others.

EDUCATION

Doctor of Philosophy in Organic Chemistry, 1975, Harvard University

Master of Science in Organic Chemistry, 1973, Harvard University

Bachelor of Science in Chemistry, 1971, UCLA. Graduated Summa Cum Laude, Phi Beta Kappa, and First in Department.

not once you have a more established career. Two good rules to follow:

1. Include only the last 15-20 years' worth of jobs. But...

2. Include all job experience that is relevant to the position you are seeking, even that which is older. Leave out that which is irrelevant, even if it's recent.

Is It Ever Okay To Lie on a Resume?

The short answer is, of course, NO. There are some creative (and widely known and acceptable) maneuvers you can do to handle problem situations like being fired. However, ultimately you will likely have to fess up. You may be tempted to include a computer skill you don't possess or claim to have that master's degree you were only three credits from finishing, but be safe and do not lie on a resume. Fact checking of dates and degrees is far too easy today. You can say that you have worked toward a degree, or that you were runner-up for a particular award, but do not claim something you didn't earn. Finally, including a few failures or warts on your resume—jobs or projects that didn't pan out—may actually be helpful. It establishes credibility and makes the rest of the resume look more honest. And if you can demonstrate that you learned from these experiences too, that demonstrates more well rounded experience. Nobody has a perfect career.

My Computer Skills Aren't Up-to-Date. How Do I Handle This?

The growth of technology has changed the way people communicate and do business. And because we work in a global economy now, it is necessary, even in non-technical positions, to have a rudimentary understanding of the Internet, e-mail, and basic word processing, spreadsheets, and desktop publishing. For those earlier in their career, list the technical skills you do have, then get going on taking that Powerpoint class. Executives may need a working familiarity with certain elements of technology, such as manufacturing technology or enterprise software, but they don't have to know how to use it, and listing such expertise is not a major requirement.

What Are the Latest Resume Gimmicks I Should Incorporate?

None. Your resume is no place to experiment with new bells and whistles. It is a professional document, not a place for neon colors, funky fonts, or anything that doesn't represent you as a consummate professional. In fact, recruiters believe that the more off-the-wall features (except for those in artistic professions), the more someone has to hide.

Some people now store their resume as part of their personal Web sites. This is acceptable, as long as you are aware that anyone can view your resume in cyberspace. You'll also still need to send hard copies of your resume, rather than submitting a cover letter directing employers to a hyperlink.

How Do I Explain Job-Hopping?

Ten years ago, job-hopping was frowned upon; now the opposite is true. Recruiters are more likely to be leery of someone who has been with only one company for a long time. On the other hand, having three jobs in one year doesn't look great either, but you can explain in your interview process why you have changed jobs and how now you are ready to settle down and find the right fit.

I've Been Laid Off. How Do I Address This?

There is no shame in being laid off. It happens. There is no need to go into detail about the layoff on your resume. You want only pieces of information on your resume that can help you. During the interview process, you can explain your situation further. If you must have the layoff on the resume, turn it into a positive: "Due to merger, stayed on to assist in transition, then accepted severance offer." Treat your previous job as if you chose to leave it. Do not badmouth your company, and be sure to list all the important experience you gained from the job.

I've Been Fired. How Do I Address This?

You do not need to say you were fired on your resume. This is something that can be discussed in the interview process. Getting to the interview process is the first step; don't take yourself out of the running by divulging too much information on your resume. But once in the interview process, do not lie. Explain what you learned by being fired, why you believe it happened and why you won't allow it to happen again. If your experience is solid, then unless you embezzled money or burned your company down, being fired won't disqualify you.

How Do I Explain Gaps in My Past Employment (Maternity Leave, Illness, Burnout)?

With today's prevalence of job-hopping, consulting gigs, and telecommuting, gaps between jobs are more common and more understandable. And the longer a person's career, the more hard-pressed a company will be to find someone without a gap during that time. Maybe you preferred not to return to work right after having your child. Or you followed your spouse to his/her new job, and you have yet to find the right position. A company is interested in your experience and your commitment to the future. Again, remember that no career is perfect. You don't have to explain gaps on your resume–you can do so in the interview process. Doing consulting or freelance work now can also help thwart a current gap.

What If I Don't Have Experience in the Field I Am Applying For?

You have more experience than you think. First look at the job listing and note the key requirements. Then find areas in your past jobs that demanded the same types of skills: motivating people, giving presentations, etc. Place this relevant experience at the top of your resume. Focus on the relevant skills, not the specific experience or history in the field or industry. Recruiters and employers are more interested in skills than history.

Do I Need An Objective Statement?

Objective statements are now considered passé because they demonstrate what a company can do for you, not what you can do for the company. They also don't focus on skills, but rather personal ambitions. Instead, use a "Profile" or "Expertise" heading with a two-to-four sentence summary of your talents. Also, be definite about your specialization (business development, sales, or marketing) so a recruiter can more quickly match you with a job. With recruiters, you'll have to generalize, because they will likely send your resume to many firms. If applying for a job you find on your own, you might want to amend your profile to fit a particular job.

Should My Resume Be Chronological or Functional?

Chronological resumes order your past jobs with the most recent first. Functional resumes group work experience according to skill set. With some very rare exceptions, use the chronological resume. Functional resumes are sketchy and popular with those who have something to hide. Recruiters and hiring managers know this. Better to creatively handle difficult career situations in a chronological resume than to raise a red flag by using a functional resume.

Should I Include My Volunteer Experience and Personal Interests?

The farther along you are in your career, the less need to point these out. However, if they are relevant to the job, or taught you an important skill you did not learn at your previous job, yes, include them—but only if they truly reflect another dimension of your skills and capabilities. Don't put them on your resume as space-filler. If you are an accomplished triathlete or serve as an officer of a local nonprofit, yes. If you like to collect beer cans, no.

Where Do I List My Education?

Unless you have schooling from a particularly prestigious institution (MBA, Wharton), list education at the bottom of your resume. You should list your academic concentration, honors or awards achieved, and significant extracurricular achievements. Don't list your fraternity or sorority house or your varsity letters. You do not need to list your grade point average. Education should be listed even if irrelevant to a job—there is many an art history major in today's executive suites. Professional credentials and certifications should also be listed. If you don't have a college or professional education it's probably best to omit the education portion altogether.

Should I Include My Salary Requirements and References?

Absolutely not! You may divulge your salary requirements to your recruiter in a cover letter or in conversation, but not on your resume, which can be forwarded to employers. Do not include references either. It's understood that you can provide them to the recruiter or employer at a later date. The phrase "References available upon request" is passé. However, if Martha Stewart or Robert Redford can speak well of you, then yes, you might want to include them on a separate "Addenda" page with their names and contact information.

RESUMES FOR DIFFERENT FIELDS

Of course, nothing is ever as easy as it seems, and resumes are no exception. While a resume in any field should follow basic guidance like "honest" and "concise," some fields have slightly different needs from applicants' resumes. For example, scientific resumes tend to be longer and often have additional headings to allow for explanations of projects, experiments, and publications. Political resumes and sales resumes will be bolder and brag even more than the standard resume. Academic resumes (often called CVs or curriculum vitae) can be 15 pages long or more. If your next job falls into a field that is outside general business, consider consulting some resume books or a professional for assistance in formatting your resume correctly.

Using a Resume Writer

Having a professional look over your resume certainly can't hurt. The important part is finding a true professional, someone who is reputable and does not make guarantees or charge exorbitant rates. Call your local university's career counseling department, or check with the Professional Association of Resume Writers and Career Coaches for a resume writer in your area. (http://www.parw.com/home.html)

Resumes vs. Executive Resumes

Just as recruiters for mid-level professionals and senior executives may differ, so will their resumes. Executive resumes tend to be longer and more conversational in tone, with fewer tools like bullet points or descriptions of volunteer work. There is more of a narrative feeling to them, often with full paragraphs describing a job rather than short, punchy bullet points. They focus strictly on an executive's experience, while those below executive level simply have not yet had time in their careers to accumulate such business acumen. Executive resumes should be long on experience and ability to deal with situations, reason, make decisions, and lead an organization. They are more about working with people and organizations, both inside and outside the company, and less about numbers and specific accomplishments.

COVER LETTERS

Candidates often put a great deal of effort into their resume, then throw together a cover letter with little attention or thought. Rather than try to do what a cover letter is for–to briefly introduce yourself and garner interest in your overall accomplishment–they waste time and space with useless fluff and worse–rehash their resume. Then at the end, they casually ask for a phone call if the recruiter is interested. Doesn't work.

You have to remember that a recruiter or employer will see your cover letter before the resume. It is not an insignificant document. The good news is that it does not have to be a lengthy essay about your hopes and dreams.

"Short, short, and short," says Mark Jaffe. The cover letter should be no longer than four paragraphs, and some have been well received with three lines. Rather than a copy of paragraphs from the resume, it should have a strong opening and then hit the major highlights of your career and how they can help the related companies. Do not open with "Hello, my name is…" but with a direct mention of your accomplishments and/or your connection with the particular company: "Dear Mr. Faber: Jim Parks suggested I contact you. I have the experience you need to achieve a 30 percent increase in your patio furniture sales."

John H. Patton
3144 Chester Avenue
Los Angeles, CA 90036
213-555-3442

October 16, 2002

Mr. James Snyder, President
Jefferson Furnishings
3422 Rosewood Court, Suite B-16
San Francisco, CA 94112

Dear Mr. Snyder:

After considerable success and 17 years in the furnishings market, I am seeking a new challenge to pursue. Your vice president, Martin Kemper, suggested I contact you for such an opportunity.

In my last operating position, I created a 20% increase in gross revenues in an industry that has struggled with a 30% decline in recent months. The company was under new and inexperienced management, as well as encroaching local competition, but my team and I resolved the problems to add 15% to gross and 7.2% to margins.

In my current position, I implemented nine new national accounts with major companies, as well as solidified relationships with our established business partners, generating $1.7 million in new business. I can manage problems from both sides and create greater profits through attention to both revenues and cost containment.

I would like to have a meeting with you to get acquainted. I believe it will help you achieve the type of management you would like. I'll call your office on Wednesday, October 21 to make arrangements. Thank you for your consideration, and I look forward to meeting you.

Sincerely,

Roger F. Stein

Figure 8-2. Sample Executive Cover Letter

The idea of a cover letter is to serve as a brief teaser. Let your resume and the interview do the ultimate talking about you.

A few more points to note:

- If you need extreme privacy in your relations with this recruiter, be sure to note that in your cover letter.

- While salary and reference lists may be requested, you do not have to include this information in your cover letter (or your resume). You can state that you will provide the information in an interview, and when you do, give your honest salary history and requirements (one phone call can expose a lie about salary history). Be sure to give correct information for your references as well, with as many contact numbers as possible to ease the task of your recruiter's having to find them.

- Close the deal. Don't sign off the letter with "I look forward to hearing from you." Rather, make a definite commitment: "I'll contact you Monday morning at 10 a.m. Please advise if some other time would work better." Or: "I'll be in town on June 15th. Would it be possible to get together then?"

Figure 8.2 is a good sample cover letter.

From what's been shared here, you may well still not be comfortable with the task of assembling your job search documents. There are many sources of reference material available. Some recruiters may help you directly, some may point you to the best resources. Most major bookstores have good, understandable, up-to-date treatments in the career section filled with examples to help you build your resume and cover letter.

CHAPTER 9
ACCEPTING A NEW POSITION

What saves a person is to take a step. Then another step.
– Antoine de Saint-Exupery

y now you have come a long way. Is it end of the road, or just the beginning? You have established a relationship with a recruiter, rewritten your resume, and have interviewed for at least one job. Finally, your hard work has come to fruition: the recruiter contacts you with news of an official offer.

GETTING THE JOB OFFER

You should be proud to receive a job offer, even if it is for a job you ultimately decide not to take. It is no small feat to reach this point. An offer means you have presented yourself and your skills well, have proven how your past experience can be an asset to a future position, and your references have given positive feedback about you. You have been chosen over several other worthy candidates. It also means that the recruiter has done well by you. This entire process usually takes three to four months, so you have been patient as well.

Depending on where you are in your career, you may never have been in this position before. A company actually paying someone else to come and specially hire you? It can be flattering, but also intimidating, to be chosen for a job offer, especially if it's a big promotion or a move into a new type of position or industry. Add to that having to make the decision whether or not to relocate or to undergo a tough negotiation, and you may feel that deciding what to do with the offer may be the hardest part of the job search yet!

Now either the recruiter or the hiring manager has given you the good news. You may also receive an official letter, explaining the details of your new job, your title, salary, benefits and any other perks. What do you do now?

You Are Not Alone

You may be excited and ready to take the offer as is. Or, perhaps you have discovered that you would not like to work for this company after all. Maybe you want to accept it but make a few amendments first. Or maybe you just need time to think about what is best for you and your family. While a job offer is great news, it can bring with it major dilemmas.

Whatever your decision, you have a partner to give you guidance–your recruiter. Their job is not over once the company decides to hire you. It is important to use your recruiter as a resource and be willing to work with him or her and trust their judgment and advice. True, they are working for the client company, but it is in their best interest to strike a deal that makes everyone happy.

In fact, at this stage, your relationships are most important. Relationships–with your recruiter, your new employer, your former manager–should be foremost in your mind as you undergo the job-changing process. How you present yourself and communicate your needs will affect you not only this time around, but also in future job changes too (and as you have discovered, those are likely to happen again!).

Yes, No or Maybe?

The easiest scenario: you are thrilled with the offer as it is and want to accept the job right away. This is fine. There is no need for the old-school thinking of stalling and demanding more simply to look tough. If the offer is truly what you want (and contrary to what you might have been taught, some companies do give their best offer up front), go ahead and accept. However, it's still not a bad idea to ask for a day to look over the offer and make certain you are not forgetting anything.

Also remember that if you like the offer, you do not need to rush and say "yes" to avoid losing the job to another ready candidate. It doesn't work this way. The company has chosen you first for a reason. It is perfectly common and understandable to ask for two or three days to consider an offer. You may just want a night to sleep on it, or perhaps you need to discuss the offer with your family. At the very least, you will want a chance to discuss the offer with your recruiter if they weren't the one to deliver the news. They can give you guidance as to how much time you can take. Tell the employer that you need some time to consider the offer, and give them a concrete day and time by which you will give them a definite answer.

You may even receive more than one offer at once, or you have one offer from one company but expect an offer from a different company soon. Time can be a critical factor here, and this is a judgment call for you. But it is acceptable to tell your recruiter or hiring manager that another company would like to hire you, and you need time to consider both offers. You're a great candidate – why wouldn't you have more than one offer? Remember to work with your recruiter honestly and fairly; if you have received an offer outside of their efforts, they aren't someone you need to play games with. They might even be able to help you get an even better deal. Just be sure not to keep either company waiting too long as there are other candidates in the wings. And don't lie and say you have offers on the table when you don't; you could risk losing a good, real offer by looking greedy or difficult or simply by taking too much time.

You may also realize that while the offer is good, this job is not something you would like to pursue after all. Maybe you have discovered during the interview process that you would not like this line of work, or perhaps you didn't feel as if you would fit into the company. (And certainly tell the recruiter if anything offensive or illegal occurs with the company during your interview process!) Again, it's okay to say no. Just be honest with your recruiter as to why you are declining; ideally, you have already raised these issues with him or her in the past so they will not be a surprise now.

Most often a job offer will have some things you like, some things you don't. It falls into the maybe category. So begins the negotiation process.

SO, WHAT AM I WORTH?

Before you can negotiate, you need a clear idea of what you are worth in today's marketplace. And don't just rely on salary calculators; do research and keep up with salary trends in your chosen field. The better prepared you are, the more likely you can get a salary you like. After all, your would-be employer may not be totally aware of salary trends, and they are representing the company's interests, not yours.

Your recruiter can help you determine where you and your skills currently fit into the marketplace. They already know about you and your history as well as the job offer you have received; they may also have worksheets to help you inventory and align all the qualities you have to offer.

Determining your worth takes some research, but you might be surprised how much you could go for, particularly in strong job markets. Compensation packages at one time only included salary and stock options, but now there are many things you need to consider, things that are part of your inventory, earned either in your previous jobs or on your own:

- Previous titles
- Your degrees/education/on-the-job training
- Company car
- Health benefits/gym membership
- Technology (cell phones, laptop, etc.)
- Consulting/speaking experience
- Professional memberships
- Relocation assistance
- Vacation time or sabbaticals

Factors like these not only give you more clout as you enter negotiations but also are good to keep in mind when an otherwise great job has a lower-than-expected salary. Often these side benefits can make up for a lower salary in the long run.

Keep in mind, too, that these variables may differ in worth according to region and industry. You should take into consideration where your next job will be and what the cost of living is for that area as you calculate your value.

Finally, as you make your list, decide what items you simply must have in your next job, those you can live without, and those that have room for negotiation. Do you really need to work from home once a week, or can you instead ask for a week more of vacation time? Can you forego a signing bonus in light of an early performance review? Perhaps tuition assistance toward your MBA will make up for a lower annual base salary.

Again, a recruiter can be your ace in the hole for determining your worth. They can help you determine which perks are most important, the ones worth fighting for. They can also help you be realistic about what you don't want to push for. They are a part of this process and only stand to gain if you do. Work with them, and the recruiter will help you get the best possible offer without overstepping your bounds. For upper-level managers and executives, the recruiter can be extremely helpful, as compensation packages can be very complex, including not only the above but stock-option packages, yearly bonuses, and executive tax preparation. Recruiters have navigated through these packages before, know what to look for and can help assess how the offered package stacks up. There are many factors to take into consideration in a compensation package, but the recruiter knows them all, so you don't have to. At this stage, the recruiter acts a little like your agent—but remember, they work on both sides of the table in the interest of getting a deal done.

NEGOTIATING

Even people who have been through the negotiation process before can still find it uncomfortable. The word "negotiation" conjures up images of dark-suited men in a wood-paneled, smoke-filled room, pushing envelopes back and forth across the table.

But really, negotiation can be a fairly open and even friendly process, with a lot of wiggle room—many factors that can be discussed. Everyone wants an ideal situation in the end, so think of negotiation with a positive attitude. Also, with a recruiter, you have someone not only to advise you, but even help do the dirty work of presenting your requests. If you dislike making monetary demands or don't trust yourself to be firm on areas that are important to you, a recruiter can take the offer and present it to the hiring company without you. Their position helps you in two ways: it relieves you of having to face the employer, and you know if they are comfortable with your demands, chances are the hiring company will be too.

Negotiation Points

Many people think salary is the only area that can be negotiated, but there are many variables to work with. Often people become so focused on negotiating salary that they will not only lose the offer, but also get the salary they want at the cost of other benefits. (Not to mention make them look greedy. What happened to that easygoing guy or gal from the interview process?) Different people, say, a married parent of three vs. a single person just of college, can benefit from different compensation packages, involving factors such as these:

Health Benefits. With today's mounting healthcare costs, a job with a solid health benefits program is worth consideration against a job with a higher salary but with benefits that are partial or don't begin until a certain amount of time is accrued. There are also other perks that can help, like a gym on-site, or free memberships to area gyms. What fees would you save there as opposed to having to pay for your own workouts?

Family Care. Many companies today offer assistance with child and elder care; some even have childcare facilities on-site. This is a great perk that should not be overlooked in light of salary.

Stock Options and Deferred Compensation. In years past, stock options generally applied only to executives. However, in the 1990s, when Internet companies were booming, even secretaries were given stock options in addition to (or in lieu of) salary as new companies hoped their service or product would be the next big thing. Of course, many of these companies failed, leaving people with no salary and little, if any, worth to their stock options. Companies new and old are still offering stock options, but they can be a tricky business.

Today, stock options can certainly be a nice plus, especially if the company is steady and the options vest quickly. Research the value of the company you are considering, or enlist the help of a financial planner to determine the worth of stock packages. However, this is one time, for safety's sake, you may want to put salary first.

Deferred compensation plans–retirement plans–can be one of the most important variables. For most mid-level executives, there is a 401(k) or similar retirement plan available. You should check the matching and vesting policies. For higher-level executives, there is a vast assortment of qualified and non-qualified deferred compensation available, including such items as special insurance policies, profit sharing and bonus arrangements, stock purchase plans, and so forth. Think of your job offer in terms of the future, not just for what you can get right now. A lower salary and a solid deferred comp plan with tax-deferred company contributions can prove more valuable in the long run.

Relocation Assistance. Relocation can have a major impact on a new job, especially if you are moving to a market with a higher cost of living. You must calculate what it will cost, not only to move there (which can run in the thousands of dollars), but how to live with a lifestyle in which you and your family are comfortable. Consider asking for relocation assistance, be it paying for your move, giving you a hotel suite for the first few months, or helping your spouse to find a job in the new location. These are all very common and worthwhile arrangements, so don't be afraid to inquire about them.

Company Car. A company car, or reimbursement for expenses incurred in using your own vehicle, can be a negotiating point if your job requires frequent travel. Also be sure to find out what sort of travel awards programs the company has and if you can earn those miles for personal use. If you're at the highest levels, of course, company and charter aircraft privileges, first-class travel, and so forth are important.

Sign-On Bonus. Sign-on bonuses are lump sums paid upfront when someone joins a company. These can be a great negotiating tool when the salary isn't quite up to par, and it's not necessarily the company's fault. Perhaps a higher salary that you want and deserve does not fit within the company's current salary structure, or maybe it is a great job but in an area with a lower cost of living. A signing bonus of some of the difference could help you get started while you prove your worth and possibly revisit a higher salary six months later.

Early Performance Review. Like the sign-on bonus, an early performance review can be a tool to help get your salary up to your standards sooner. Rather than working the standard year before the first review, arrange for a meeting in three months or six months with the possibility of a raise according to your performance.

Title. While it may not have any more current monetary value, you might be able to get a better title with more clout. Ultimately, it can help boost you in the hierarchy at that company or get you a better offer at a future job. However, be sure to research what level each title is at the new company. While you may have been a vice president at your old company, that might be considered only middle-management level at the new company.

Work with your recruiter to decide what makes the best compensation package for you. If the current offer isn't enough, you don't have to take it. The key in negotiations is to ask for most, but not necessarily all, of what you want, but then both sides should be willing to compromise. If you push too hard on a particular point, you may lose the offer. But if you don't push hard enough, you may feel undervalued, and neither way is how you want to start with a new company. Trust the recruiter's judgment—they get paid off the package they design for you, so they aren't going to let anything slide. Nor are they going to push too hard; the two of you are something of a team, and you need to work together.

Once you have received the job, the recruiter can still act as a buffer for you. Since you and your new company may have some concerns at the beginning, the recruiter can deliver information between the two of you in a courteous, professional manner. Recruiters want you and the company to be satisfied with the search; their success depends on it.

LEAVING YOUR CURRENT JOB

If you dislike your current job, your impulse is probably to make a break for the front door the moment you sign the offer for your new position. Again, relationships are a factor here, though, as you never know whose paths you might cross again. It is in your best interest to be discreet, mature and helpful as you transition from one job to another, if for no other reason than to make yourself look good (and to get in a few goodbye gifts).

Before You Make Your Announcement

You'll want to begin your transition even before you tell people—in fact, even before you actually get the new job. You'll want to have copies stored of all your paperwork, contacts, performance reviews, and work examples, both in hard copy and on your home computer. In case you are escorted (usually a security formality) from your desk the day you announce you are taking a new position, you want already to have copies of all your files (and continue maintaining these records from now on). You may also want to begin discreetly removing personal items and pictures from your desk.

Be thinking about how you can help replace yourself, either by training a current co-worker, writing up guides to your work, or making hiring suggestions for a new candidate. This will help soften the blow when you make your announcement.

Don't start making calls to your recruiter or new company within earshot of others. Even though you have inked a new deal, you still want to continue being professional and a hard worker. You want your old company to be sorry you are leaving, not glad you are gone. This will also help in the future should you need a reference from your old job—how you act in the next two weeks can make all the difference in the impression you leave behind.

Making the Announcement

You'll want to do this in person, not by phone or e-mail. And you certainly do not want to call from home and say you are not coming in anymore. No matter how much you might like to exact a bit of revenge on an old boss, it can only come back to haunt you later. Sit down with him or her in person and state that you are leaving. You do not owe them specifics as to why, or that you have been using a recruiter, but simply that you have been given an opportunity that can help move your career in the right direction. You can be honest now, or later in an exit interview, about specific issues you had with the company, but refrain from badmouthing or casting blame.

Be prepared for possibly being asked to leave that very day. Or, you may very well receive a counteroffer. But before you accept a higher salary, consider your situation. If you have already signed the offer from your recruiter and new company, you are really left with only two choices: take the new job as planned, or take the counteroffer. At this point you cannot negotiate any further with your new company and you will risk looking greedy if you do. And if you do take the counteroffer, you are risking the bitterness of your recruiter and would-be new company. Ask yourself why you want to leave your current situation in the first place—will more money really make a difference?

After the Announcement

Once you have announced your news, continue to be a good employee. Work hard and stay focused on your current company's goals. Help in finding a replacement for your job. Keep personal calls to a minimum and certainly do not openly discuss how much happier you will be at your new position and how you can't wait to get out of there.

Especially important is getting down to your HR office. Do it now and begin closing out your paperwork—health benefits, 401(k) rollovers, exit interviews, and the like. Do not wait because you will be busy getting adjusted at your new job and you may let an important form slip through the cracks, or miss a deadline for moving your retirement account. You do not want to lose time to invest your money.

HOW TO MAINTAIN YOUR RECRUITER RELATIONSHIP

Now that you have started your new job, you will be busy, of course, getting up to speed learning the ropes and freeing yourself from your previous position. It's easy to let your relationship with your recruiter fall by the wayside. But don't make that mistake. Just as you have probably learned (maybe the hard way) the value of maintaining a network of colleagues, you want to make certain you stay on your recruiter's radar screen. You might as well go ahead and laminate a permanent rolodex card for your recruiter, and plan to check in every few months. No, it's still not a good idea to call and just chat, but you do want to keep the lines of communication open for several reasons.

What If You Don't Like the New Job?

If, after a solid amount of time at the new job, you find that you are still restless, you may want to let the recruiter know that you would like to be considered again for employment. It won't hurt the recruiter's feelings if your new job doesn't work out (as long as you hold up your end of the bargain by being a good employee who puts in your due time before making any rash decisions). In fact, he or she needs to know about factors that don't turn out the way you had planned. This helps in hiring for that company in the future. Be especially certain to notify your recruiter about any illegal activities: discrimination, violence or other criminal acts. And if you do like the new job, be sure to tell the recruiter that as well. Much as with a job interview, it is considered in very good taste to send a nice thank you note expressing gratitude for his or her services.

Paying the Piper

The relationship with a recruiter is a two-way street. Now that they have helped you find a job with a great compensation package, you may be called upon to help them from time to time. Try and provide client referrals when you can, but only people you would recommend yourself. And should you stumble across one on your own, let your recruiter know. There is no better way to stay in good graces, as well as to have an excuse to call once in awhile, than to report a potential hire.

Happy Trails

Congratulations, you are now equipped with the skills for two areas: your current career, and that of career seeker. The latter may be even more important than the job you already do. We have said it before, but let us reiterate: Always be willing to seek better positions for yourself, even while you are happy where you are. You never know what the next day will bring or what other glorious opportunities await you, and you don't want to wait (again) until it is too late to find out. So maintain your relationships with your recruiter, former co-workers and your network of colleagues, family, and friends. Keep yourself updated on the market and your value in it. And always be open to new opportunities, or willing to pass them on to others. With this attitude, you will always recruit success.

PART 4
APPENDICES

THE LEXICON OF EXECUTIVE RECRUITING

A Glossary of Terms Used in the Professional Process of Searching for Executives

Compiled and published by Executive Recruiter News,
the independent newsletter of the executive search profession.

Annual Retainer. A form of volume discounting of executive search services. Client agrees to pay so much a month, quarter or year, thereby establishing a credit account against which specific placements are billed. Encourages long-term relationships for greater efficiency, lower marketing costs, improved client service.

Appraisal Interview. See EVALUATION OF CANDIDATES.

Association of Executive Search Consultants (AESC). Organized in 1959 as the Association of Executive Recruiting Consultants, Inc., this association brought together leading executive search consultants who established strict requirements for membership and standards of ethical practice for their professional field. AESC membership identifies the consultant who is not only pledged to these high standards but who is also accredited by his professional peers to conduct his practice with professional competence and integrity. The association office is at 500 Fifth Avenue, Suite 930, New York, NY 10110, www.aesc.org.

Blockages. Places where recruiters cannot look for candidates to fill a position. Usually refers to corporations that are off-limits because they are, or recently have been, clients of the search firm (see Off-Limits Policy).

Boutique. Typically small executive search firm that specializes in one or more relatively narrow niches in contrast to presenting a generalist image.

Bundling. Relatively new term describing the talents required in today's "super executive" who is brought in to replace two or three others and is expected to reflect a "bundling" of all their attributes. Bad for search in that there are fewer jobs to fill, but good because super-execs are scarce & hard to find, requiring professional search.

Candidate. A person who survives extensive screening, reference-checking and interviewing and is to be presented to the client for the position to be filled.

Candidate Blockages. Candidates who may not be considered for a position because they are active candidates in another search.

Candidate Reports. Summaries prepared on each final candidate that usually include a complete employment history, personal biographical data, appraisal of qualifications, and initial reference information. Data is verified and submitted to the client for examination prior to the first meeting with the candidate. Where possible, search consultants prefer to make their presentation in person so as to permit maximum exchange of ideas and information.

Career Counselors. Firms or individuals offering services to individuals. Some are legitimate but many are not. Some have been forced out of business by state Attorneys General for failure to meet promises: many have been investigated. (Be wary of claims in blaring ads in Wall Street Journal, N.Y. Times, etc.) Services can include psychological testing, resume preparation, interview training, job-search planning, etc. Fees can run from modest to $10,000! Read fine print in contracts and check with legal counsel before making a down payment or signing anything. Dealing with a small, local counselor on a 1-1 basis is usually best and least expensive. Extreme caution is advised.

Client. Organization sponsoring and paying the recruiter for a search.

Client Anonymity. One of the principal reasons for using executive search. Client identity is usually not revealed to prospective candidates until well along in the process, except in general terms.

Client Block. See OFF-LIMITS POLICY.

Code of Ethics. Every profession has found it necessary to establish a code of ethics as a necessary part of the process of self-discipline, and to protect the interests of clients and assure them of fair treatment. A code of professional ethics helps the practitioner determine the propriety of his conduct in his professional relationships. It indicates the kind of professional posture the practitioner must develop and maintain if he is to succeed. It gives the clients and potential clients a basis for feeling confident that the professional person desires to serve them well, and places services ahead of financial reward. It gives clients assurance that the professional person will do his work in conformity with professional standards of competence, independence and integrity. The AESC Code of Ethics is followed by many executive recruiting consultants in North America.

Compensation Package. Total compensation can include various elements other than salary for senior executives: typically a mix of deferred income, incentive bonus, profit-sharing, stock options, tax shelters (or some type of compensation that permits estate-building), thrift plans, pension plans, life insurance, health insurance, long-term disability insurance, dental insurance, tuition assistance, payment for personal and family medical and dental expenses, cars, club memberships, loans, joining bonus and other perquisites (including, increasingly, some form of hiring bonus).

Completion Rate. Percentage of retained searches that result in a hire. Estimated to be as low as 60 percent, claimed by some to be 100 percent (be wary of the latter: no one is perfect, and the imponderables/intangibles in a search are many). Greatly affected by client lassitude in interviewing and following up with candidates, changes (written and subtle) in job specifications, internal client politics, organizational changes, etc., as well as by recruiter performance and effectiveness.

Confidential Search. There are times when it is important for the client to conduct confidential searches. When secrecy is necessary, it is virtually impossible to handle a search from within the organization. For example, a company may want to introduce a whole new line of products or acquire a new product or company before competitors learn about it. In such cases, a recruiter can work effectively on its behalf without disclosing its identity until the final stages of the search. The company can make its selection and announce its plans after the new executive is on board.

Keeping a search totally confidential requires considerable discipline and skill on the part of both client and recruiter. Once the client has been identified to the top two or three candidates, both the client and the recruiter must be ready and able to move fast to make a final decision and a public announcement. This is the only way to avoid possible leaks, and it requires careful coordination.

"Con-tainer" Search. Fee arrangement that combines elements of retainer and contingency methods of payment. Usually involves an initiation payment and progress payment(s) that may not be refundable, with a "success" or "completion" portion due only on actual hiring.

Contingency Search. The search consultant who uses the contingent fee approach must fill the position before his fee is paid by the client.

Dehiring. See OUTPLACEMENT.

Directory of Executive Recruiters. Listing published by Kennedy Information since 1971. Thousands of names and addresses, with salary minimums and areas of specialty (indexed by management function, industry and geography). Updated annually.

Employment Agency. Employment agencies normally limit their efforts to representing individuals who are actively looking for new employment opportunities within the local area. When an organization contacts an agency to fill a specific job opening, the agency usually reviews its files for applications from people with appropriate backgrounds and may place ads in local newspapers to attract additional applicants.

Employment agencies often try to place their applicants in any of a large number of local organizations because they are paid by the individual applicant or employer only if a placement is made. They make the majority of their placements in the lower salary ranges. Their payment is a fee based on the employee's starting salary.

Their fees may be regulated by the state and frequently follow the pattern of a 5 percent minimum plus 1 percent for each $1,000 of the annual salary of the individual employed, up to a maximum of 20-30 percent. Some states also permit an advance fee or charge to the individual who lists himself with an employment agency. The line between Fee Paid Employment Agency and Contingency Recruiter is sometimes very difficult to draw.

Employment Agreement. When the client organization and candidate have agreed on terms of employment, it is usually important to put these into writing as a protection to both parties. The employment agreement may take the form of a formal agreement or letter to the new executive spelling out everything discussed and agreed upon: job specifications, reporting relationships, base salary, benefits, moving costs, etc. The executive will then reply, either by telephone or letter, and the deal will be settled.

Equal Opportunity Act. An Equal Employment Opportunity Commission was established in Washington, D.C. in 1964 to prevent employment discrimination. (The Roosevelt Administration established a similar organization to prevent such discrimination during World War II.) Although the law demands that women and other minority employees be considered for executive positions at various levels, most organizations, for example, lack candidates with both the education and experience required for such positions. Consequently, a growing number of these organizations must look outside for qualified individuals from the relatively small pool of qualified middle and top managers. To help such companies, some search firms have set up special departments to recruit such executives. Others specialize in this field.

Evaluation of Candidates. At a convenient time and place, the recruiter interviews the prospective candidate to verify the original information gathered during the process of sourcing and researching, to examine his background in depth, and to determine if the personal chemistry will be appropriate.

These appraisal interviews develop an in-depth picture of each candidate: his employment background, business philosophy, career objectives, potential and personality characteristics. Education and employment are verified, and a reference investigation is made of past performance. From the group of prospective candidates evaluated, several of the best-qualified are selected for introduction to the client. During this phase of an engagement, the recruiter's breadth of background, depth of insight and sound judgment are critical.

Evaluation of Executive Recruiter. What benchmarks should the client use in evaluating the recruiter's performance over a period of time? They include professionalism, results, adequate communications, realistic costs, proper staffing of assignments and timing of assignments.

Executive Assimilation Process. The process of integrating the new executive into the organization. See SHAKEDOWN EXERCISE.

Executive Clearing House. These are information centers whose basic function is to bring together employers and candidates for positions on an informational basis. They collect information from two sources: individuals interested in a position, and employers or their search consultants seeking executives to fill specific positions. The information concerning the person and the position is classified and put into a mechanized or computerized retrieval system. Both the individual and the employer are expected to share the cost of these information centers. Companies may pay either a standard amount per position or per year, or a placement fee if and when they employ a person referred by the Clearing House. Some of these have been computerized into Job Banks or Registries of one sort or another. Caution is advised.

Executive Recruiting. The service performed for a fee by independent and objective persons or a group of consultants organized as a firm or similar entity. Executive recruiters help managers of client organizations identify and appraise executives well-qualified to fill specific management positions in commerce, industry, government, and the nonprofit field. Their fees are paid by the organizations that retain them.

This highly specialized area of the management consulting profession started as a normal service rendered by general management consulting firms. Executive recruiting has experienced rapid growth since the end of World War II, both in the United States and abroad. There are hundreds of consultants (most of whom refer to themselves as "firms") that handle executive search either as a specialty or in conjunction with other forms of consulting work.

Executive recruiting firms, also known as executive search consultants, generally bill their clients monthly as the search progresses and deduct these payments from the total fee, frequently up to 35 percent of the first year's total compensation. Some may use other methods of billing such as a regular per diem, or a flat fee, plus out-of-pocket expenses.

The true role of the executive recruiting consultant is not that of a glorified pirate, body-snatcher, headhunter, or any other erroneous label frequently applied to him or her.

Executive recruiting consultants are usually willing to receive resumes from executives seeking new job opportunities, but they are not in a position to help executives find jobs.

Executive Referral. Euphemism for RESUME FLOATING to former or present client.

Executive Search. Synonym for EXECUTIVE RECRUITING, although some feel strongly that "search" better describes the process and identifies its major thrust.

Expenses. Additions to the search fee intended to compensate the recruiter for out-of-pocket payments incurred specifically for a given search (i.e. telephone calls, special directories or subscriptions, candidate & recruiter travel, etc). An item to be carefully monitored by the diligent client, as some search firms tend to "make money" on expenses (double-billing for travel involving two clients, for example). Other firms attempt to recover ordinary administrative expenses. A variable item on the search firm's invoice, but bears watching and documentation of over 15-20 percent of the fee.

Fair Credit Reporting Acts. Legislation to amend general business law regarding procedures for securing information about individuals seeking commercial credit, loans, jobs, etc. Also covers the confidentiality, accuracy, relevancy and proper use of such information. Can affect the reference-checking aspect of executive recruiting significantly. Regulations vary widely from state to state.

Fallout. Term popularly used to describe the following condition: after a placement has been made (or during the assignment), the client decides to hire one or more additional candidates who surfaced and were recommended by the recruiter. Some search firms demand full fee for each such additional hire: others will not accept a fee. Most frequently a matter of negotiation dependent on the time frame, client relations, etc. See PLACEMENT, MULTIPLE.

Fee. The total fee paid by the client to an executive recruiter for a search assignment. Most recruiters these days charge clients 30-33 percent of the first year's total compensation for the executive hired, plus out-of-pocket expenses. Thus, if the new executive is paid $50,000 base salary and no bonus or incentive, the client's fee would be about $15,000 regardless of the billing method, plus 10 to 25 percent of the professional fee for out-of-pocket expenses. Retainer recruiters are paid for their services whether or not a placement is made. See METHODS OF BILLING, FRONT-END RETAINER, INVOICING ARRANGEMENT and REIMBURSABLE EXPENSES.

Front-End Retainer. During the course of a search, clients are invoiced monthly for agreed-upon fees, plus out-of-pocket expenses. These monthly installments generally range from one-third to one-fourth of the total fee involved. They are sometimes called "front-end retainers" and are credited toward the total fee when the individual is employed. Usually a final billing for any remaining fee is rendered at that time. Retainer recruiters require a payment before commencing a search. This is also called a "front-end retainer."

Greenlighting. When companies merge, this is the signal given to the manager to start looking, because his counterpart in the other company will assume his role for the combined firm.

Guarantee. Promise by the search firm to replace a failed candidate within a certain period of time (usually one year), especially if caused by negligence on the recruiter's part. Search is usually reinstated for expenses only.

Handwriting Analysis. (Graphology) A controversial selection technique pioneered in Germany and in occasional use elsewhere as another tool to help predict candidate performance and fit.

Headhunter. Formerly pejorative term for executive recruiter, still only passively accepted by professionals in the field... currently used more in a jocular and light-hearted sense than critically... even voiced occasionally by some headhunters themselves! (Other labels, far less in evidence today, have included "body- snatcher," "pirate," etc.)

Hiring Bonus. A one-time payment originally intended to compensate a joining executive for extra expenses occasioned by a major move. Now viewed somewhat more broadly, though not quite like a professional ball-player "signing bonus," nonetheless the comparison had been made! The concept includes, for example, recompense for "lost" bonuses at the company the executive is leaving. It can also be a device to compensate for lower salary scales in the hiring company. A hiring or joining bonus, then, is whatever it takes in addition to total compensation to convince the candidate to join. The amount can range from a few thousand to over a million dollars, sometimes paid half on joining and half six months later.

Interview. Another word for both preliminary and appraisal interviews which are conducted for the purpose of assessing prospective candidates.

Interview, Stress. This is a Nazi-like technique once promoted by a recruiter in New York City as applicable in executive recruiting. Through it, the prospective candidate is bludgeoned with insulting remarks until he finally loses his temper, thus presumably revealing his true inner self. Few (if any) recruiters use such techniques.

Invoicing Arrangement. Regardless of the type of fee structure used by the recruiter, the client should understand the invoicing arrangement in advance. Many recruiters require a payment before commencing the search. Others will do much of the preliminary work involved in a search before sending the first invoice. Invoices for professional fees and out-of-pocket expenses may be payable monthly for three to four months or may require payment at certain periods during the search, usually with the final payment upon completion of the search.

Job Counselors. See CAREER COUNSELORS and OUTPLACEMENT.

Job Description. This describes the client position to be filled and outlines the desired characteristics and experience that the executive being sought should possess. When approved by the client, the "specs" become the guidelines for the search.

Leaving Money on the Table. Outside search consultant's lament when placed executive gets higher first-year compensation than was estimated and fee was fixed, not percentage.

Length of Recruiting Assignment. The average recruiting assignment takes three to four months from the initial meeting with the client until the candidate is finally selected. Once a new executive is selected, it may take two to four weeks or more before he or she actually reports to work. An assignment may take as little as a month or two if everything goes right, but this is rare. On the other hand, a search may take six months to a year. When it lasts that long, chances are that the position was impossible to fill, the specifications were changed, the client was not available to meet candidates or didn't really want to fill the position, the recruiter miscalculated, or something else out of the ordinary happened.

Licensing. Many years ago, when immigrant laborers were taken advantage of by unethical employment agencies, most states enacted legislation to protect individuals by licensing and control of such agencies. Thus employment agencies are licensed today; executive recruiters are generally not. As employment agencies move into fee-paid and retainer work, the line becomes more difficult to draw. Many states now write specific exemptions for executive recruiters, citing salary minimums and the fact that the individual does not pay a fee.

Lobbing. Following a shootout, the losing firm "lobs" a resume to the client, showing the kind of candidate the losing firm would have recruited had it been given the assignment.

Methods of Billing. The most commonly used methods of calculating the professional fees charged for executive search services are:
- A fixed percentage fee, usually 30 to 33 percent of the first year's agreed-upon total compensation of the executive recruited.

- A flat fee, fixed in advance on the basis of estimated time and difficulty of the search.
- A retainer fee for professional services over a stated period of time.
- A straight time formula, based on actual time spent on the search, but sometimes governed by an agreed- to-maximum.
- A per-diem or hourly fee for any candidate appraised and recommended by the recruiter and hired by the client.

In addition to the fee, there are also expenses. These are mainly for travel and communications, and they will vary, depending on the complexity of the search and the distances between client, recruiter and candidates. It is customary for clients to pay for candidates' travel to interviews. See FEE and REIMBURSABLE EXPENSES.

Off-Limits Policy. A key issue in executive search. Refers to the recruiter agreeing not to approach executives in the client organization. Factors are definition of "client" and time: the whole corporation (e.g., General Motors) or the division the search was done for (Chevrolet), or some even more specific entity (Truck Division, Northeast Region)... and for one year, two, three?

Some large firms say they can't "afford" a strict Off-Limits policy because it reduces the universe from which they can draw and gets extremely complicated ("client" served by the San Francisco or Zurich office, how significant a client, etc.). Small firms magnanimously offer "full" worldwide client protection because it doesn't really affect their business.

Whether this is an ethical or trade practice or business issue, it is extremely important to have it fully and mutually understood, preferably in writing, at the outset of a search assignment.

Outplacement. When executives are fired or dropped by various kinds of organizations today, they are often referred to outplacement consultants. These specialized consultants analyze their abilities and counsel them on how to prepare resumes and find new careers. Outplacement consultants work for and are always paid by the firing organization. A few serve both companies and displaced executives, and there is in such circumstances a potential conflict of interest. The Association of Executive Search Consultants (AESC) bars its members from offering outplacement services for the same reason.

Person Specification. A synonym for JOB DESCRIPTION

Personal Chemistry. There is a rough analogy between mixing chemicals and mixing executives at the top level. By combining executives, an organization can achieve synergy, or neutralization, or can produce explosions. The daily newspapers verify this chemical analogy as it operates in the executive suite.

   The search for a new executive is part of a process of organization change, often with traumatic implications. Preparing for this change and tackling the inherent integration problems are essential if the needs of the individual and group are to be met.

   In their evaluation of prospective candidates, professional recruiters try hard to determine whether the personal chemistry will be appropriate. A few recruiters help clients integrate new executives into the organization on as firm a footing as possible by means of formal programs. Interpersonal breakdowns can create enormous organizational cost, and it is important to anticipate and head them off.

Placement. The act of an executive re- cruiter in filling a client position.

Placement, Multiple. When a recruiter is searching for a top-level executive, he or she frequently interviews candidates who are not exactly right for the position, but who may be of interest to the client for another position. When the client fills a secondary opening with a candidate presented to him for the primary position, it is called a secondary or multiple placement. This happens often enough so that the recruiter should spell out the details in his confirmation letter before commencing the search. Some recruiters charge a full fee; others reduce their fee for a secondary placement because their research effort time devoted to the placement has been absorbed by the primary search. See FALLOUT.

Privacy. An infrequently used synonym for confidential search. It is also used to refer to the various privacy acts and legislation protecting the individual.

Professional Practice Guidelines. These are standards of good practice for the guidance of executive recruiters. They make for equitable and satisfactory client relationships and contribute to success in recruiting.

(See the AESC Code of Ethics and Professional Practice Guidelines for specific standards of good practice.)

Progress Payments. Monthly payments made to the recruiter by the client for agreed-upon fees, plus out-of-pocket expenses, during the course of the search. Frequently cited as a key difference between Contingency and Retainer Search.

Proposals, Letters of Agreement and Contracts. Each recruiting assignment should have as its base point a formal written instrument (usually a letter of agreement or proposal) between the recruiter and the client. It should accurately describe the terms of the assignment. Unwritten agreements often lead to misunderstandings and dissatisfaction on the part of one or both of the parties. The written agreement should be specific on all pertinent points: job or position specifications, responsibilities of each party, amount of fee, method of payment, time limits involved and any other pertinent points of agreement.

Psychological Testing. Professional search consultants develop their own evaluation methods. Formal psychological evaluation is almost always left to the client's discretion. If a client has doubts about the fitness of a candidate, psychological evaluation may be indicated. But it is not likely that the search consultant will use psychological testing as part of its own selection process.

Ratcheting. The temptation faced by retainer recruiters charging on a percentage basis: the higher the salary at which the candidate is hired, the higher the fee (even a hint of conflict of interest in such instances is eliminated when charged on fixed-fee basis).

Records Maintenance. Professional recruiters have clear policies known to their staffs regarding the retention of records and coding in compliance with existing laws and regulations on federal and state levels, together with the spirit of the various privacy acts and legislation protecting the individual.

Recruiting Costs. See FEE and METHODS OF BILLING.

Recruitment Advertising. Professional recruiters feel that advertising with regard to a particular assignment should be done judiciously, and only with the approval of the client. It should state the position clearly and be used with discretion. Absolute honesty in statements and actions should be observed in the text of the advertisement.

In Europe and Canada, advertising is commonly used in the executive search process. Sometimes this is called Executive Selection; at other times the terms are interchangeable.

References. Persons to whom a recruiter refers for testimony as to a candidate's character, background, abilities, etc.

Executive recruiters usually take references proffered by candidates only as a starting point. They then confidentially seek out former superiors, subordinates, peers, colleagues, vendors, suppliers, etc., to get an independent and objective evaluation of the candidate. See below.

Reference Checking. After intensive interviews with the candidates (but before introduction to the client) the recruiter will begin to check references. Initially the recruiter will be limited to references provided by the candidates. These are likely to be favorable. However, from these references the recruiter will obtain others (known in recruiting as second-generation references) who will be likely to provide a more objective picture of the candidates. These references include such persons as social contacts, professors, business associates and former roommates.

This initial checking of references is a delicate area and must be done with prudence. It is vital that the candidate not be embarrassed or have his current job jeopardized as a result of these checks. In addition, the client often wants the search to remain confidential at this stage.

For these reasons, it is customary to defer an in-depth development of reference information until mutuality of interest has been determined.

Reference investigation and reporting should be conducted with the candidate's prior knowledge; within the spirit and intent of applicable federal and/or state laws and regulations; with persons considered knowledgeable about the candidate and whose information can be cross-checked for objectivity and reliability; and with respect for the personal and professional privacy of all parties concerned. References today are rarely in writing, usually in the form of telephone notes.

Referral Service. Most large banks in metropolitan areas provide a referral service for executives, especially in financial and general management fields. They provide this service at no cost to their customers, and the executives are generally seeking a new position. Often, banks will recommend executives for senior positions if their particular skills will strengthen the customer's position. Large law firms sometimes provide a referral service to their clients. Trade associations and professional organizations also refer names of members who are actively in the job market at no cost to job seekers or interested companies. In addition, placement offices of most universities offer a free referral service, and many graduate schools of business help place their alumni.

Reimbursable Expenses. All recruiters incur out-of-pocket expenses in their day- to-day search activities. Typically, there are travel expenses for both recruiter and candidate, related costs for hotels, meals, long-distance telephone calls, printing and other related costs. Some recruiters charge for their reimbursable expenses at cost while others may add a service charge. Some charge for secretarial, research and other support services while other recruiters absorb part or all of the expenses.

Reimbursable expenses may run from 10 percent to 25 percent of the professional fee or more, depending on such factors as length of assignment, location of client and the majority of candidates, number of offices used by the recruiter and salary range of the position being filled. International searches covering several countries obviously incur higher expenses.

Replacement Guarantee. See GUARANTEE.

Research. The foundation of professional recruiting is research. All well-established recruiting consultants maintain research facilities to develop background information about industries, companies, and key executives. In a rapidly changing business environment, constant research is the principal guarantee against superficial or haphazard research work.

Resource. Someone who can possibly recommend a candidate for a specific opening.

Resume. A brief account of personal and educational experience and qualifications of a job applicant. The resume is the first formal contact between a company and a potential employee, and in some ways it is the most critical. Personnel officers in most major corporations can usually give only 20 to 30 seconds of attention for each of the many resumes they see every day. So, to make the best impression, an applicant's resume must be constructed in such a way that it provides the most pertinent information about him or her in the simplest and most easily digestible form. The information should be brief, complete & easily accessible.

Resume Floating. Frowned-upon practice of sending resumes to a potential hiring organization without a contractual search assignment, in hope of a "hit"... banned by AESC as "inappropriate."

Retained Search. Retained search is one in which a client retains a recruiter to identify and appraise executives well-qualified to fill a specific management position. An initial down payment is followed by progress payments, and the full fee may have been paid before the position is actually filled.

Retainer. A retainer fee (usually paid monthly) for professional services for an agreed-upon period of time.

Rusing. Using subterfuge to obtain information, typically posing as editor or researcher or personal friend to get information on executive names, titles, etc., in research phase, banned by AESC as unethical. See UNETHICAL RESEARCH.

Search Process, The. The task of identifying and appraising well-qualified executives is painstaking and time-consuming and must be governed by an orderly approach, consisting of several major steps or phases, if it is to be successful. These steps represent the broad phases of a typical search assignment and identify the major areas of activity involved in the work that recruiters do for clients.

These steps are interrelated and interdependent, but they are often adapted and modified by search consultants as they work out their own approaches to client engagements. The professional search process does not depend on luck, shortcuts, or gimmicks, but on a step-by-step procedure whereby a list of potentially suitable executives is reduced to several uniquely qualified candidates. In outline form, the successful search consultant must: meet with the client to discuss the engagement in depth; develop a strategy or search plan; review files and previous search assignments; contact candidates and evaluate them; check references and participate in negotiations; and follow-up with the client and executive to see how things are going.

The aim is not merely to produce qualified candidates (which is relatively easy) but the very best candidates available.

Second Generation Reference. See REFERENCE CHECKING.

Shakedown Exercise. This exercise or process sometimes involves getting the new executive and his or her boss together in a one- or two-day session with a behavioral psychologist before the new executive reports to work. It is based on the premise that the end of the search process is only the beginning of the more rigorous, more critical process of integration into the new organization. In these sessions, each nails down precisely what each is expecting of the other. The purpose of the shakedown exercise is to bridge the gap between promise and performance. This approach, with its emphasis on behavioral science techniques, is not yet common practice in recruiting.

Shootout. Popular term for competition that finds several search firms making new-business presentations to a potential client. Increasingly used, to the recruiter's chagrin, by sophisticated, cost-conscious or short-sighted clients who sometimes fail to see the value in long-term professional relationships.

Source. Person or organization that can suggest possible candidates to a recruiter during a search.

Specialist vs Generalist. Increasingly, clients demand a certain amount of industry or functional knowledge from the executive recruiter. Exclusive practices have sprung up in banking, healthcare, training, hi-tech, finance, etc. Yet there is always the demand, in addition (especially at higher executive levels), for the generalist viewpoint. How else, for example, can an executive with consumer products marketing experience in soft drinks be found for the personal computer company that has decided it needs this type of leadership?

Some industries lend themselves to recruiter specialization, i.e., those with a large number of non-competing units nationally (banks, hospitals). Others, with a high concentration of firms (automobiles, for example) do not lend themselves to specialization. The determinant is adherence to a professional Off-Limits policy. See OFF-LIMITS POLICY.

Stick Rate. Term sometimes used to describe effectiveness of executive-position matches, whether through search or otherwise. No real statistics yet on whether searched executives last longer in new posts. Not to be confused, however, with success rate (i.e., underperformers can sometimes stay in the job for a long time!).

Stopper. When a search firm hears another search firm may get an assignment, it sends over a few resumes as "stoppers." See LOBBING.

Super-Executive. Manager who combines the talents and experience of the two or three people he or she is replacing. See BUNDLING.

Suspect. A person identified in a preliminary way as a possible candidate to fill a search assignment.

Total Compensation. See COMPENSATION PACKAGE.

Types of Executive Recruiters. These include independent individual recruiters and recruiting firms, executive recruiting divisions of management consultant firms and certified public accounting firms, and internal recruiting departments in companies.

Unbundling. Separating the key elements of full search and offering them individually, i.e., research, interviewing, etc., sometimes "demanded" by aggressive clients, sometimes offered aggressively by entrepreneurial recruiters seeking additional revenues.

Unethical Research. Certain practices, such as phone-sourcing and "research" techniques which involve misrepresenting the caller or purpose of the call, are unprofessional and are not tolerated by professional recruiters regardless of whether they are employed by subcontractors or the search consultant himself. Such practices undermine client confidence in the integrity and professional reliability of recruiters. See RUSING.

CODE OF ETHICS AND PROFESSIONAL PRACTICE GUIDELINES

The Association of Executive Search Consultants (AESC)

The Association of Executive Search Consultants (AESC) is an association of leading retained executive search consulting firms worldwide. Dating from its inception in 1959, the AESC has sought to promote high standards of professionalism among retained executive search consultants. In furtherance of this aim, AESC adopted a Code of Ethics in 1977, and a set of Professional Practice Guidelines in 1984. In 1996, with the advice of a panel of AESC member firm leaders and outside experts, the AESC revised and updated both the Code and the Professional Practice Guidelines to reflect important developments in the profession and the business environment. In 2002, a similar panel once again revised and updated the Professional Practice Guidelines.

"Retained executive search consulting" is a specialized form of senior-level management consulting conducted through an exclusive engagement and on a predetermined retainer-fee basis. Its purpose is to assist executives of a client organization in defining executive positions, identifying well-qualified and motivated candidates, and selecting those best suited through comprehensive, quality-assured search processes.

Executive search is widely recognized as an indispensable service to organizations worldwide and is generally built on relationships rather than discrete transactions. The services provided by executive search consultants are an integral part of the process of building and maintaining corporate, nonprofit and government clients. Like professionals in the fields of law, public accounting and general management consulting, executive search consultants have a profound influence on the organizations they serve.

AESC and its members recognize that outstanding professional service rests on the quality and integrity of relationships with clients, candidates, employees and the public. Executive search consulting firms depend on all of these groups for their continuing success, and to each group they have important responsibilities.

Clients

AESC members are partners with their clients in a consultative process aimed at selecting organizational leaders. As "leadership" can have many meanings, the professional search consultant identifies the client's specific needs and unique culture as essential elements in recruiting appropriate leaders for client organizations.

Candidates

AESC members maintain professional relationships with candidates and treat them with respect at all times. AESC members regard honesty, objectivity, accuracy and confidentiality as fundamental to their relationships with candidates.

Consultants

AESC members strive to attract and develop their own talent, building the knowledge and experience that will guide the profession into the future. Recognizing the importance of training and education to this process, AESC members provide opportunities for consultants, research professionals and other staff to improve their skills and capabilities. AESC and its member firms are partners in professional development.

The Public

AESC members understand the importance of public trust in the executive search profession. Professional search consultants stay abreast of socioeconomic developments in the communities they serve, and recognize the need to respond to contemporary developments such as changing demographics, new technologies and changes in the employment relationship. AESC's mission includes understanding these changes and taking constructive positions on public policy issues that affect the executive search profession, client organizations and the public.

The AESC's updated Code of Ethics clarifies the fundamental principles that guide executive search consultants in performing their duties and conducting their relationships with these constituencies. The Professional Practice Guidelines represent the AESC's view of contemporary best practices that exemplify the standards of professionalism expected of executive search consultants into the 21st Century. Underlying these principles and best practices is the expectation that AESC members will articulate and define clearly for clients the terms of their relationship and the members' commitment to perform their work professionally.

CODE OF ETHICS

AESC member firms, in order to perform their duties responsibly, are guided by the folowing ethical principles which reflect fundamental values of the retained executive search consulting profession. The AESC is committed to educating its members about the application of these principles.

	AESC members will:
Professionalism:	conduct their activities in a manner that reflects favorably on the profession.
Integrity:	conduct their business activities with integrity and avoid conduct that is deceptive or misleading.
Competence:	perform all search consulting assignments competently, and with an appropriate degree of knowledge, thoroughness and urgency.
Objectivity:	exercise objective and impartial judgment in each search consulting assignment, giving due consideration to all relevant facts.
Accuracy:	strive to be accurate in all communications with clients and candidates and encourage them to exchange relevant and accurate information.

Conflicts of Interest:	avoid, or resolve through disclosure and waiver, conflicts of interest.
Confidentiality:	respect confidential information entrusted to them by clients and candidates.
Loyalty:	serve their clients loyally and protect client interests when performing assignments.
Equal Opportunity:	support equal opportunity in employment and objectively evaluate all qualified candidates.
Public Interest:	conduct their activities with respect for the public interest.

PROFESSIONAL PRACTICE GUIDELINES

Preamble

The Association of Executive Search Consultants (AESC), as a worldwide association of retained executive search consulting firms, strives to enhance the professionalism of its members. Accordingly, AESC has developed the following Professional Practice Guide- lines to assist AESC member firms in their business relationships with clients, candidates and the public around the world. The AESC may amend these guidelines from time to time as the profession evolves and adapts to developments in business practice, technology and the law.

Relationships between AESC Members and Their Clients

AESC members are partners with their clients in a consultative process aimed at selecting organizational leaders. Success in these partnerships depends upon a strong mutual commitment to the task at hand as well as mutual trust, candor and responsiveness by each party as the search progresses. The AESC recommends that, in order to avoid misunderstandings later, agreements between clients and member firms concerning conduct of the search and other significant matters should be put into writing.

Accepting Client Assignments

Outstanding client service begins with a full understanding of the client organization, its business needs and the position to be filled. An AESC member should:

- Accept only those assignments that a member is qualified to undertake on the basis of the member's knowledge of the client's needs and the member's ability to perform the specific assignment.
- Disclose promptly conflicts of interest known to the AESC member and accept assignments only if all affected parties have expressly agreed to waive any conflict.
- Develop an understanding with the client that, among other things, makes clear the organizational entity that is defined as the client organization, the fees and expenses to be charged, and any ongoing assurances or guarantees relating to fulfillment of the assignment.
- Agree with the client concerning any "off-limits" restrictions or other related policies that govern when and how the member may recruit from the defined client organization in the future.
- Agree with the client on what information about the position in question will be made available to candidates and sources during the search, when this information will be released, and in what form.
- Advise the client when advertising is required by law or is a recommended strategy for the particular search assignment.

Performing Client Assignments

Members should serve their clients with integrity and objectivity, making every effort to conduct search consulting activities on the basis of impartial consideration of relevant facts. Specifically, an AESC member should:

- Conduct a focused search for qualified candidates consistent with a search strategy agreed upon with the client.
- Develop with full client involvement and approval a comprehensive job description for each search engagement and make this available to candidates before they are presented for interview with the client.

- Thoroughly evaluate potential candidates before presenting them for an interview with the client. Such evaluation normally includes in-depth interviews in person or by videoconferencing, appropriate preliminary inquiries into references and background, and a careful assessment of the candidate's strengths and weaknesses against the specification for the proposed position. Clients should be advised when circumstances require a modified approach.
- Agree with the client as to what reference and background checks need to be conducted on finalist candidates, what elements these checks should cover, how extensive they should be and who will perform them. (See the AESC's Reference & Background Checking.)
- Present information about the candidate to the client honestly and factually and include any reservations concerning the candidate that are pertinent to the position.
- Advise the client promptly and offer alternative courses of action if it becomes apparent that no qualified candidates can be presented, or that the length of the search will differ considerably from that originally specified.
- Withdraw from the assignment if a member determines that a client has characterized its organization falsely or misled candidates and is unwilling to rectify the situation.
- Refrain from the presentation of resumes in the absence of an existing client relationship.

Preserving the Confidentiality of Client Information

AESC members should use their best efforts to protect confidential information concerning their clients. Specifically, a member should:

- Use confidential information received from clients only for purposes of conducting the assignment.
- Disclose such confidential information only to those individuals within the firm or to those appropriately qualified/interested candidates who have a need to know the information.
- Not use such confidential information for personal gain, nor provide inside information to any other parties for their personal gain.

Avoiding Conflicts of Interest

AESC members have an ethical obligation to avoid conflicts of interest with their clients. For example, a member should:

- Refuse or withdraw from an assignment upon learning of conditions that impair the member's ability to perform services properly, including actual or potential conflicts of interest unless all affected parties expressly agree to waive the conflict.
- Provide to clients the member's undivided loyalty as an advocate and professional advisor in the process of negotiating with finalist candidates. Only in exceptional circumstances, and only with agreement in advance of all affected parties, may candidates be presented to more than one client simultaneously.
- Inform clients of business or personal relationships with candidates that might affect or appear to affect the member's objectivity in conducting the assignment.
- Not accept payment for assisting an individual in securing employment.

Relationships Between AESC Members and Candidates

Although a member's primary relationship is with the client, member firms also seek to establish professional relationships with candidates. These relationships should be characterized by honesty, objectivity, accuracy and respect for confidentiality. In building such relationships, a member should:

- Explain the relationships that exist between the parties involved in a retainer-based search consulting engagement, and in particular the rights and obligations of the candidate in the process.
- Provide candidates with relevant and accurate information about the client organization and the position.
- Encourage candidates to provide accurate information about their qualifications.

  Upon learning that a candidate has misled the client or member regarding his or her qualifications, reject the candidate unless the client, candidate and member agree that the candidacy should continue following disclosure of the facts.

- Present to clients accurate and relevant information about candidates, and otherwise maintain the confidentiality of information provided by prospective and actual candidates.
- Only provide an individual's confidential resume or other confidential data with the individual's prior consent, and in the context of an existing client relationship.
- Advise prospects and candidates of the status and disposition of their candidacies in a timely fashion.
- Explain that only in exceptional circumstances may an individual be presented on more than one search simultaneously, and then only if all involved parties agree.
- Advise candidates that, so long as they remain employed by the client organization, the member firm may not approach them as a candidate for a future search without the express permission of the client.

Relationships Between AESC Members and Their Contractors

AESC members sometimes rely on contractors and subcontractors to assist in the search process. Services may be subcontracted but responsibility for them cannot be. A member should:

- Inform its contractors and subcontractors in writing that they should adhere to the AESC's Code of Ethics and Professional Practice Guidelines.
- Avoid contractors and subcontractors whose practices are inconsistent with the standards of professionalism expected of AESC members.

Relationships Between AESC Members and the Public

AESC members should recognize the importance of public trust and confidence in their profession and seek to serve their clients in a manner consistent with the public interest, taking into account differing legal contexts in different countries. Therefore, a member should:

- Observe the principles of equal opportunity in employment and avoid unlawful discrimination against qualified candidates.
- Promote and advertise member firm services in a professional and accurate manner.
- Conduct relations with the media so as to reflect favorably upon clients, the AESC, and the executive search consulting profession.

Steps to Effective Reference and Background Checking

The taking of reference and background checks is a critical part of the search process. In order to avoid misunderstandings or problems at a later date the AESC considers it is the responsibility of the search consultant to clarify who will conduct reference and background checks, and to ensure that all parties involved, i.e., consultant, client and/or specialist third parties, understand their roles and responsibilities in the process. The following guidelines are intended to help AESC member firms, clients and candidates better understand the definitions and processes involved in this phase of a search consulting engagement. However, member firms operate in many different countries and these guidelines should not be interpreted to contradict specific national legal requirements.

Definitions

Reference Check: comments, oral or written, from current and past employers or colleagues concerning a candidate's strengths and weaknesses vis-a-vis the proposed position.

Employment History Check: verification of dates, positions and responsibilities during a candidate's professional career.

Educational and Professional Credentials Check: verification of a candidate's college attendance, awarded degrees and professional certification.

Criminal Record Check: a check of a candidate's name against appropriate district, regional and/or national criminal records.

Civil Record Check: a check of a candidate's name against appropriate civil records.

Background Check: this is a broader term often used to include all checks with the exception of the reference check.

Media Check: a check, often employing the Internet, to see if a candidate has been mentioned in newspapers or other media during the past several years.

Reference Checks

Reference Checking is a way to expand understanding of candidates' skills and experience through the opinions of those who have worked with them. The intention is to build up a comprehensive picture of a candidate and to validate or challenge conclusions that the search consultant and client initially may have reached.

References customarily are conducted by search firms both in the preliminary stages of a search, and, more comprehensively, in the final stages of a search as an individual becomes the favored candidate. At this latter stage clients may also choose to conduct references on the candidate. Since, at this point, discretion and confidentiality issues can be particularly delicate, AESC recommends that this collaborative process be carefully orchestrated by the search consultant.

The AESC does not recommend a specific number of references to be taken nor how far back in a candidate's professional career references should go. Rather, the specific reference checking process to be employed should be discussed and agreed upon between the search consultant and the client since the circumstances of each search engagement are unique.

Background Checks

Background checks seek to ensure the accuracy of more objective data such as employment chronology and educational credentials. They also seek to ensure that the candidate has no civil or criminal history that would preclude successful fulfillment of the responsibilities of the proposed position.

Many large corporations routinely conduct such background checks on all senior executive appointees, along with other screenings such as medical and drug testing. Some do this in-house while others employ specialist organizations to conduct the checks on their behalf.

AESC recommends that the search consultant explicitly agree with the client as to who will assume responsibility for such background checks. Regardless of who conducts them the search consultant should ensure that there is agreement with the client as to the level of checking and degree of thoroughness appropriate to the engagement.

AESC: WHAT TO EXPECT FROM A SEARCH FIRM

The following is reprinted from the July 2001 issue of Executive Recruiter News.

The Association of Executive Search Consultants (AESC) releases a roadmap of sorts for hiring companies to better understand the complexities of retaining and working with search firms and maximizing their return on the investment.

The release comes at a time when a number of firms are discounting search fees and improving the quality of their service to compete for a depressed market for new searches and client partnerships.

It aims to educate the consumer of high-end executive search services about their rights and obligations as a client and how to distinguish between good service and bad. The following is a sampling of some of the AESC's prescriptions for a successful engagement between a retained executive search firm and its client. (Note that the following directives talk directly to the client's best interests.)

■ **The executive search firm shall provide a high-level consultative relationship.**
"Retained executive search consulting" is defined as a specialized form of management consulting, conducted through an exclusive engagement and on a pre-determined retainer-fee basis. Its purpose is to assist your organization in defining executive positions, identifying well-qualified and motivated candidates, and selecting those best suited through comprehensive, quality assured search processes.

In addition to locating high quality candidates, your search firm should also provide information and feedback that not only helps direct your search for executive talent but can also be used to run your business more effectively. This feedback includes:

- Knowledge of the industry in which the search will be conducted, including availability of candidates, comparative assessments of those candidates, and remuneration levels.
- General market research regarding how your organization is perceived in the market, what your competitors are doing, and what kind of recruiting strategies may or may not be working at any given point in time.

Do not expect a 50-page market research report for your retainer fee. But the search firm should give you a reasonable overview of market conditions and the general perception of your organization in the marketplace for talent.

■ **The executive search firm shall demonstrate a clear understanding of the position, the company and the objectives of the search.**

In order to conduct a successful search, the consultant must have a crystal clear understanding of the position to be filled, the requirements of the job and your company's culture. Accordingly, you should insist on receiving a report that details the consultant's understanding of:

- Your desired level and type of experience
- The background, education and technical skills needed to successfully perform the position
- Responsibilities of the position
- Any interpersonal skills needed

Good search firms will do more than just feed back the job description you present them. They will proactively help you develop, modify and refine your own understanding of the position. To help with this critical step, give your search consultant access to all those who participate in the selection process and encourage them to provide full disclosure regarding the position to be filled. Because the job description represents the bedrock of a successful search, you have a reciprocal obligation to notify the consultant any time circumstances (either internal or external) require a change in the position or the type of person you're looking for. Be aware that a major change in search specifications may require a change in fees.

■ **The executive search firm shall hold your information
   in strict confidentiality.**

By its very nature, an executive search requires you to divulge highly sensitive information about your organization. The search consultant must treat any and all information you give them with the utmost confidentiality. At the same time, the consultant cannot conduct an effective search without making some information available to potential candidates. To protect your interests, however, the search consultant should guarantee that he or she will:

- Use confidential client information only for the purposes of conducting the assignment.
- Disclose client information only to others within the search firm (who may be supporting the consultant on this assignment) or potential candidates who have a need to know the information.
- Never use confidential information for personal gain or provide that information to third parties for their personal gain.

■ **The executive search firm shall provide you with regular, detailed
   status reports on the progress of the search.**

Depending on the position to be filled, the availability of talent and a host of other factors, a successful search can take anywhere from a few weeks to several months. To keep you up-to-date, the search firm should provide ongoing progress reports that include:

- The companies at which the consultant has tried to target candidates
- The market response to the search
- Obstacles to identifying or attracting candidates
- Candidates currently being developed

The search firm should update you regularly, either by phone, fax, e-mail, written report or some combination of all four. Let your consultant know your preferences.

■ **The executive search firm shall present qualified candidates who fit the position and the culture of your organization.**

The consultant should present you with a range of qualified potential candidates, whom he or she has thoroughly assessed and interviewed. The consultant should be able to discuss each candidate's:

- Experience level and significant achievements relative to the position to be filled
- Education and background
- Intellectual, interpersonal and motivation competencies
- Personal strengths and weaknesses with respect to the position to be filled
- Perceived cultural fit
- Interest in the position
- Remuneration and financial expectations

In presenting candidates, either individually or in a "short list," you should expect the consultant to discuss the interviewing arrangements and other issues that can affect the critical interviewing process. Immediately after you have interviewed candidates, your search consultant should solicit your comments and feedback and help you conduct comparative candidate assessment and analysis. They should complete and transmit to you the verification of credentials and reference checks.

If it becomes apparent that the search will take considerably longer than expected or that it may not yield an acceptable range of candidates, the consultant should inform you as soon as possible and discuss alternative courses of action.

■ **The executive search firm shall help you negotiate with the final candidate, representing both parties with skill, integrity and a high degree of professionalism.**

Once you have selected a final candidate, the consultant's role changes from that of search agent to negotiator and communicator. At this point, the consultant's primary function is to help you bring the candidate on board in a manner that facilitates a long and successful stay with your organization. This includes:

- Acting as an intermediary between you and the candidate regarding compensation, benefits and other conditions of employment
- Feeding back to you any reservations or concerns the candidate may have about accepting the position
- Helping the candidate to assess the opportunity
- Working with both sides to create a "win" for everyone

Although the consultant represents your interests first and foremost, he or she must also remain sensitive to the needs and concerns of the candidate. To do otherwise significantly reduces the chances of a successful hire. In addition, representing both parties with integrity and professionalism ensures two important outcomes:

- The candidate comes aboard feeling that he or she has been treated fairly
- The search enhances your company's reputation in the marketplace

Remember that your candidates are also very busy professionals who have sacrificed valuable time to talk with you. Furthermore, they did not solicit this opportunity; it was presented to them.

IACPR PROFESSIONAL RECRUITING GUIDELINES

The International Association of Corporate and Professional Recruitment

▪ Purpose
To develop, establish and promote ethical standards and practices among the IACPR membership.

▪ Privileged Information
It is vital to the executive search process that exchange of information between the search firm and the company be held in confidence. The Executive Search Consultant must have access to sensitive information such as organizational strengths and weaknesses, marketing plans, new product developments and strategic plans in order to set the benchmarks for qualifying candidates. The use of such information for any other purpose is prohibited. Similarly, company representatives must treat information from a search firm with confidentiality such as candidate profiles, search strategies, search firm policies and procedures, and data gleaned through candidate interviews.

▪ Defined Limits
Executive Search Consultants will agree with the client what constitutes the "client organization" and will not recruit nor cause to be recruited any person from the defined organization for a mutually agreed upon period

after the completion of an assignment for the client organization. Search firms are obliged to notify a prospective client in advance of any companies appropriate to the search that will not be used due to prior client obligations.

■ Reference Checking

A feeling of trust must be preserved and cultivated between an Executive Search Consultant and a potential candidate. Reference checking without the knowledge and permission of the candidate, while sometimes expedient, is nevertheless a disservice to the candidate, unprofessional and is also unlawful.

■ Discrimination

No members of IACPR will permit candidate discrimination based on age, sex, religion, race, or country of origin or handicap, except when addressing an imbalance by affirmative action.

■ Professional Conduct

Each member of IACPR assumes the responsibility for maintaining ethical standards and projecting an image of professionalism. Members should refrain from making derogatory comments that adversely affect the interest of the Association or individual members or which conflicts with the purpose and standards of the Association.

IACPR PROFESSIONAL RECRUITING COMMITMENT TO CANDIDATES

- A candidate will be informed by the Executive Search Consultant of the role of the search firm in the assignment, the nature of the engagement, and how the search process is likely to evolve.
- A candidate has the right to accurate information from the search consultant and/or corporate recruiter, negative as well as positive, about the position, company, hiring executive, and business conditions.
- A candidate can expect confidentiality and discretion at all times. Specific information obtained by the search consultant during discussions with the candidate may not be disclosed to the client if the candidate specifically so requests.
- A candidate must be made aware, however, that the Executive Search Consultant can choose not to present a candidate based on a judgement that the candidate is not qualified or appropriate for the position.
- A candidate will be told by the Executive Search Consultant and/or corporate recruiter the title, specifications of the position, reporting relationship, location, background of the company, and responsibilities of the position prior to a first interview with the hiring executive.

- A candidate will be kept informed of the status of his or her potential candidacy on a timely and candid basis by the search consultant or corporate recruiter.

- A candidate should expect that the Executive Search Consultant and/or corporate recruiter, or another company executive will not check references without the candidate's approval or do anything that might otherwise jeopardize the candidate's present position.

- A candidate should be informed of the fact, when appropriate, that an offer may be contingent upon successfull completion of reference checks, special testing or any other conditions of employment.

- A candidate should expect that an Executive Search Consultant and/or corporate recruiter will objectively communicate his opinion of the impact on the individual's career of joining the company in the specified position.

- A candidate who is not ultimately offered the position can expect that all files will be kept confidential by the Executive Search Consultant and/or corporate client. Resumes will not be sent to another client or elsewhere in the organization without the candidate's prior approval.

- In accordance with the Fair Credit Reporting Act, a candidate who is not offered the position wherein reference checks were used as the determinant to this end may request and will be provided any applicable written documentation.

- A candidate will be informed promptly by the Executive Search Consultant and/or corporate recruiter of the client's selection decision.

- A candidate should expect to continue to communicate with Executive Search Consultant and/or corporate recruiter for at least six months after joining the company to ensure that any adjustment problems on either side are properly handled.

Notes

Notes

Notes

Notes

Notes

Notes